A PLACE
on the
WATER

A PLACE
o n   t h e
WATER

An Angler's Reflections on Home

JERRY DENNIS
Illustrations by GLENN WOLFF

ST. MARTIN'S PRESS ➤ NEW YORK

Design by Judith A. Stagnitto

Library of Congress Cataloging-in-Publication Data

Dennis, Jerry.
    A place on the water : an angler's reflections on home / Jerry Dennis ; illustrated by Glenn Wolff.
            p. cm.
    "A Thomas Dunne book."
    ISBN 0-312-09811-1
    1. Fishing—Michigan. 2. Nature stories.
3. Dennis, Jerry.
I. Title.
SH509.D46   1993
799.1'2'09774—dc20
[B]   93-21644
                                               CIP

First Edition: September 1993
10 9 8 7 6 5 4 3 2 1

for Rick

CONTENTS

ACKNOWLEDGMENTS

Most of the essays in this book first appeared, often in somewhat different form and under different titles, in the following publications:

Audubon: "Bridges"
Canoe: "My Classic Canoe," "Warring Factions," "Just Me and My Jacket"
Canoesport Journal: "Too Many Ontonagons"
Gray's Sporting Journal: "In the Buffalo Fields"
Great Lakes Quarterly: "The Demise of the Michigan Grayling"
In-Fisherman: "King Trout"
Michigan, the Sunday magazine of the *Detroit News*: "Canoeing Michigan's Wildest River"

Michigan Natural Resources Magazine: "The Trumpet on the Dead," "Haunted by the Hex" (Part 1)
Michigan Out-of-Doors: "Off-Season on the Manistee"
The New York Times: "A Big Two-Hearted Pilgrimage," "Haunted by the Hex" (Part 2), "Sturgeon, On the Ice, In a Festive Mood"
Outdoor Life: "The Quickness of Trout," "A New-Moon Bass," "The Christmas Gift," "Fishing the Jam," "A Vendetta"
Sports Afield: "Nightpaddling," "A Legendary Fish," "Winter's River," "The Heebie-Jeebies," "After Rain," "The Dunes in Winter"
Trout: "Brook Trout in Traver Country"
Wildlife Conservation: "Encounter in the Cattails"

I'm indebted to many good friends for their suggestions, encouragement, and editorial counsel, but would like to give special thanks to Norris McDowell, former editor of *Michigan Natural Resources Magazine*; Debbie Behler of *Wildlife Conservation*; Susan Adams of *The New York Times*; Vin Sparano of *Outdoor Life*; Lois Wilde of *Sports Afield*; Stephen Petit, formerly of *Canoe*; and Greg Marr of *Silent Sports*. I'm grateful as well to Glenn Wolff for his meticulously rendered drawings and for being such good company on the road and on the stream. For her ruthless criticism and (mostly) unconditional support, heartfelt thanks to my favorite petite brunette canoeing and fishing partner, Gail Dennis.

A PLACE
o n   t h e
WATER

NIGHTPADDLING

mazing, the way the world grows smaller as we grow older.

When it was still very large my father would sometimes lead me through the darkness on muggy summer nights, down the hill to the lake where I spent most of the days of my early life. We had a boat moored there, a twelve-foot fiberglass skiff, aqua-green in daylight, pockmarked with scar-like patches that covered the wounds it suffered falling from a delivery truck ten years earlier in Flint, Michigan—a fall that had reduced its value considerably in the eyes of the boat dealer, though not in the eyes of my father. It was a quick, light-footed boat, and I learned to love it like a first bicycle. In the darkness, those summer nights, I sat quietly in the stern seat while my father rowed us swiftly toward the shoreline where the bass fed. To my father the night and the boat were tools utilized in his quest for fish. To me they were wonders that allowed us to drift freely over blackness, nothingness, that left us suspended miraculously in a bowl-shaped void flecked with bits of stars and worlds. It would have been terrifying if not for my father's assured presence. I watched, fascinated, as he dipped the oars, propelling us into space, and the stars fractured and tumbled away as if we were parting them from the sky.

My father always fished. He cast Jitterbugs and Hula Poppers to the shoreline, activating them into gurgling, popping, splashing creatures that largemouth bass sometimes attacked so viciously we shouted in alarm when they struck. I fished too, but without my father's passion. It was enough for me to be there, with my father, awed by the strangeness of the lake at night.

It would be ten years before the magnitude of those summer nights came back with as much force. A few weeks after graduating from high school, four friends and I set out on a long-anticipated canoeing trip to Ontario, an expedition we had inflated with so much bravado that it became a self-conscious quest for manhood. Every step of the journey was colored by the ill-formed version of machismo that only teen-aged boys sick of being ineffectual, scrawny, and pimple-ravaged can embrace. If the trip was to be an initiation, as we wanted, it was necessary to make every step of it as difficult as possible. We pooled eight dollars each, stopped at a super-market the afternoon of our departure, and purchased gro-cery bags filled with canned stew, pancake mix, powdered milk, cooking oil, and candy bars. We did not leave home until sundown, convinced we would enjoy the six-hour drive north more after dark, when we could roll down the windows and turn up the radio and let the music and our high spirits mingle with the night. We crossed the Mackinac Bridge into the Upper Peninsula with our heads out the windows, howl-ing; crossed into Sault Ste. Marie, Canada, at midnight, our mood infecting even a stern border patrol officer who asked us why we were entering Canada and what we intended to

do there and told us, as he waved us on, to catch lots of big ones for him.

After 150 miles of highway and 75 miles of gravel road and a final 15 miles of narrow, tortuous, mud-bottomed, rock-studded, two-track trail that no doubt took years off the life of my Buick Special, we came to the literal end of the road. Late in the night we stepped from the car, cramped and tired, and stood in the cool night air astonished by the sight of the lake. It was a mirror of the sky, a crystalline plane of stars. As far as we could see were stars so bright they seemed to ring like bells.

My father had warned us that the lake, where he had come often to hunt moose in the fall, was notorious for blowing up sudden high waves that could leave canoeists stranded for days. Ahead of us was a six-mile crossing of open water to a river, a tributary of the lake. Upstream on the river was a series of lakes, each more remote than the one preceding it, each inhabited by larger and more abundant northern pike. Four or five lakes upstream my father had once shot a large bull moose; its antlers hung on the wall of the family room back home. There, also, his old friend and hunting companion Clare Fewins had cast a red-and-white Daredevl from shore, hooked an enormous fish, then stood helplessly with the rod doubled while the fish ran all the line from his reel and broke off somewhere far off near the middle of the lake. By common consent, that was our destination.

Our original plan was to set up a quick camp near the car and start across the lake early in the morning. But we were much too excited for that now. We convinced ourselves it made more sense to start immediately, in the darkness, while the lake was calm. There was little need for discussion. We took down the canoes, loaded them in the glare of the car's headlights, and pushed off into the lake.

It was the same strange nonwater, poised between sky and earth, that had awed me as a child. It awed all of us, five young men with the capacity for being so loud, brutish, awkward, and mindless in one another's company that we could be blind to almost anything. But not this. It was the closest sensation to flying we had ever experienced. One stroke of a paddle and we soared across the void. The stars shone in identical dimensions, as brilliant beneath us as above us, razor-bright and crisp, with eternities apparent between them. When we paddled, ten or twelve hard strokes in succession, our faces and hands sensed motion but there were no landmarks to gauge our progress and we seemed to go nowhere. It was almost more than we could bear. We paddled, then glided, waiting until we knew by the silence that our boats no longer cut through the water.

We spent a week exploring the river on the far side of the lake. Upstream was a series of lakes strung together like a necklace of pearls. We crossed each lake to where the river entered, often over a short falls or a stretch of rapids, then searched along the shoreline until we found a portage trail that would lead us through a hundred yards or a half-mile of hemlock and spruce forest to the next lake. In the mornings we woke at dawn to go out into the mist on the lakes and cast for the giant northerns we knew lived there. One of those mornings I hooked a large fish that stayed on the bottom, shaking its head, then towed my canoe most of the way across the lake before the treble hook on the lure straightened and the fish was gone. Another morning, after the day had warmed and the mist had disappeared, we watched a bull moose step across the shallows at the far end of the lake, each step raising large, soundless billows of water to its antlers.

Now I realize that the entire week, eventful as it was, was only an anticlimax to that first night when we paddled across the lake in the darkness. Those few hours on the water had been the culmination of the journey. We had come searching for manhood, but that night we were transported to a clarity of perception usually associated with childhood. It was our last long look at the world as children.

When we were somewhere near the middle of the lake we were surrounded suddenly by the wild, uncontrolled yelping of coyotes. Their cries echoed across the water, bounding between the granite ledges ringing the shoreline. We stopped paddling, astonished, to listen. They were not the wailing, mournful howls we'd come to expect from a lifetime of Hollywood Westerns. They were more strange than that: a sequence of yelps, barks, and yips that seemed a businesslike announcement of mealtime, combined with something like joyfulness. There was silence, and we floated in absolute, silent space. Then the coyotes began again, and we could not remain silent. We answered their cries, hooting and barking in clumsy but joyful imitation. In those moments the world expanded around us until it was vast beyond any hope of comprehension, until we were sure it would never diminish and we would never grow older.

But we did, of course, and the world has become smaller. As you grow older it becomes difficult to hear coyotes with the intensity of the first experience, or to be as awestruck by the night sky reflecting on glass-still water. But there are compensations. Now there are nights when I drift with my sons in a canoe, on the same lake where my father and I fished in that old fiberglass rowboat, and watch thunderstorms so distant and low on the horizon that their sound does not reach us and only the dim, inner glow of lightning can be seen. My sons' astonishment infects me with some of the awe and wonder I remember from my own childhood.

The night has a way of shaking us from the dullness of busy days and work. It remains, no doubt, a fine metaphor for certain mysterious, elusive truths. But metaphors apply only in retrospect. At the moment we experience it, immersed in darkness on a still lake, a singular and pure appreciation is awakened: for the world, for the water, even, in moments of extreme good fortune, for ourselves.

A NEW-MOON BASS

On summer nights the large-mouth bass that had been driven into hiding all day were on patrol, and hungry. If you stood on the shore in the darkness and listened beyond the racket of belching frogs and chirping tree insects, you could sometimes hear the sudden explosive sounds of bass feeding on the surface. Small creatures were dying out there.

My father was by nature a solitary angler. He had little tolerance for companions who talked when they should have been fishing, who clattered gear in the bottom of the boat, who made sloppy, ill-planned casts. In a land of trout streams and lakes filled with northern pike and walleyes, he was an anomaly, a bass fisherman. More: He was a night fisherman.

In those days our portion of the country was not often

recognized as bass territory. Walleye fishermen on slow days sometimes trolled crankbaits along the gravel bars and caught smallmouths, but largemouth bass almost never attracted attention. They were considered an underclass, ranked below smallmouths, which were ranked below walleyes, which in turn were ranked below the brown trout and brook trout of the dry-fly streams. Largemouths were crude. Southerners called them "hogs" and "bucketmouths" and regarded them with reverence, but in northern Michigan, in the warm water of summer, many anglers believed they grew stunted and feeble-minded. They were treated little better than bloated, slightly glorified panfish.

But Dad knew better. He had begun fishing the hidden lakes in the quiet corners of Grand Traverse, Benzie, and Leelanau counties when he came home from the Army with a serious need to spend some time on the water, years before I was born. He worked his way through two or three dozen lakes and ponds, learning them the way a scholar learns obsolete languages, and when he found the lake that suited him best he made up his mind to someday own a piece of its shoreline.

He was a restless young man. During that first six months after he left the Army he held seven jobs, and was on his way to California in search of better prospects when the car he and a friend were driving broke down while they were in Grand Rapids, still in Michigan. It took all their money to get it running again. With their last tank of gas they drove to Flint, got jobs at an auto plant, and moved temporarily into a friend's apartment. After a day and a half of factory work my father quit and went to work for a company that installed radio antennas, but the company soon went bankrupt. Between jobs he met the woman who would be my mother.

In 1959 my father moved his reluctant wife and his five- and three-year-old sons from a new house in a pleasant neighborhood in Flint to a drafty, cold, spider-infested cottage on a lake in northern Michigan. He had become a police officer on the Flint City Police Department by then, but after five years he had seen far too many murder/suicides and fatal automobile accidents, and was more anxious than ever to move north and buy his place on the water. A few months after moving to the cottage my brother and I would always remember as "The Spider House," we moved to another house on the same lake; a few years later we moved again, to a larger house on a larger lake.

Dad never looked back. He went to work repairing appliances for Montgomery Ward, then selling copy machines and overhead projectors, and devoted summer evenings to the pursuit of largemouth bass.

The summer after I turned eight years old I was struck with a passion for fishing so powerful it left room for almost nothing else in my life. I remember the moment it happened. I was sitting straddling a forked branch in a maple in the yard of our house on Silver Lake, peeling an orange. The day was bright and warm, the breeze delicious. I peeled off pieces of the orange skin and dropped them one at a time, watching them fall to the ground. Some of the pieces fell straight down, others struck branches and bounced, spinning and tumbling away. I looked through the shifting, shadowy leaves of the tree toward the lake—it was blue and ruffled, and there were boats sitting motionless on it—and suddenly I longed to hold a fishing rod attached to a fish. For just a moment I felt the bucking and lunging of the fish as surely as if I was fighting a six-pound pike. I had fished many times before that, alone and with my father, but I had never been so aware of the sensations involved. The urge to duplicate that feeling was irresistible. I finished eating the orange, climbed down from the tree, and went to the lake to cast lures off our dock. I fished every day after that, all summer. Because I was too young to operate the outboard motor myself, I spent the days casting from the dock or from shore, waiting for my father to come home from work. At night I hounded him mercilessly.

He tolerated my enthusiasm the way a mature dog tolerates a new pup in the household. And I was a very energetic pup, overflowing with the joy of new life, willing to throw all thought and prudence aside for the pleasure of an exquisite hour of fishing with him. If I was not allowed to join him—very late at night, or if he was out with my uncles and there was no room in the boat—I pouted and grew petulant. But the injustice was always forgiven the next time he looked up at me and said, "Want to do some casting?"

In some ways the critics were right. Those Yankee bass did not grow especially large. Most were two or three pounds, and the six-pounders my father landed once or twice each summer were truly bragging size, or would have been if he had been the sort to brag.

But to me it made no difference that our fish could not compare to the belly-slung hogs of Texas and Florida. It was enough just to be fishing, to be immersed in darkness, surrounded by the rich, textured odors of bottomland mixed with decomposing vegetation and the acrid scent of insect repellent, listening to the chirruping sounds of night creatures surrounding the shore like a crazed, atonal symphony.

New moon was the best time. Total darkness, my father said, would make the bass secure and careless, urge them away from cover, make them more eager to investigate disturbances on the surface. In the ink-black darkness of a new-moon night a big bass would forget hard-won lessons and would be as reckless and enthusiastic as a twelve-incher. He would attack anything clumsy enough to fall on the surface of the lake, his domain.

My father's tackle box was ancient, large, and made of steel, with foldout trays divided into compartments that had been lined with sheets of cork. He owned dozens of bass plugs—red-and-white Bass-Orenos, glass-eyed Pikies, Hula Poppers—but as far as he was concerned there was only one lure for catching bass at night: the Arbogast Jitterbug. He had Jitterbugs in every size and color, but he always preferred large ones with a frog finish. Once rigged with Jitterbugs, we were set. We could pass an entire night in contentment, casting into the darkness and listening to the gurgling music of the retrieve.

I realized that night fishing was primarily an adult activity, and that it involved a world too big and potentially dan-

gerous for children. I only fished at night because my father was there. Without him I spent my time in shallow water on bright afternoons, water you could see through to the bottom, near the rowboat pulled up on shore with its oars trailing in the sand. During the day, I caught bluegills and rock bass and adolescent largemouths possessing the same degree of inexperience and eagerness as I. In the daytime I never believed I would catch a large bass. But night fishing was different. At night bass could be as large and abundant as your imagination allowed. They swam in a world so dark and mysterious, so ripe with potential, that I knew they could be caught.

One night we fished a broad, shallow bay far down the shore from our house, a place I had seldom visited at night. I knew from daytime excursions that lily pads clogged the inner shoreline, and that along one edge ancient logs and stumps formed a border above a drop-off to deep water. We moved by oar, my father in control, and progressed slowly, one stroke at a time, until we had cast our way around the perimeter of the bay, from the stumps to the lily pads to the relatively open water on the far side. It was there, near the open water, that I was introduced into the adult world of night fishing.

An extrasensory awareness sometimes emerges when you're fishing at night. I've noticed it in recent years casting streamers on rivers for trout, trolling the flats by moonlight for walleyes, probing the undercut banks of a small stream for the brown trout that live there, but it has never been so apparent or powerful as that summer night on the lake with my father. I was not a good caster. I was inexperienced and clumsy and too eager, and yet, somehow, in the darkness I could exceed my limitations. My casts were long and faultless, always landing (I imagined) at the edges of the lily pads or in the pockets between the stumps. It was too dark to see my own hand before my face yet I knew when I had made a good cast. I retrieved the lure in fits and starts, with intervals of rest that lasted as long as I could bear to wait. Looking hard into the darkness I imagined the lure so vividly—surging, gurgling across the water, leaving a V-wake of ripples pointing to it like directional arrows—that I knew when the large bass became aware of it, when it turned in the water to focus on the odd, splashing creature on the surface, when it drifted up from the bottom and away from the weeds where it had been hovering, waiting. The realization was electric, frightening. My father felt it also. He stopped reeling, perhaps stopped breathing. Even the shore creatures seemed to sense the intention of the bass and quieted in anticipation.

I gave the Jitterbug one more twitch, a mere tightening of the line that sent the tiniest ripple of life into the water, and suddenly I wanted to yank the lure out of the water. I wanted to be safely on shore, in our house, in a room bright with lamps and a blue television screen. I did not want the drama of the night or the terrible expectancy of knowing that something large and violent was about to attack. I was afraid of the moment when the silence would be shattered by the strike and my father would shout "Whoa!" or "There!" while I shouted something far less articulate and reared back on my rod in reflex and fear.

Then, at that very moment, while I feared that it would happen, the water blew up.

I struck, reeled madly to be sure there was no slack, then struck again to set the hook, as I had been taught. By the sound and the volume of water displaced and now the heavy weight against the rod, I was sure it was not an ordinary bass. My father reeled his lure and line from the water.

"Keep the rod high," he said.

It ran, surging deep, and I knew I did not want to fight this fish. It was simply too big. I reeled futilely, the drag slipping while line was pulled out by the fish. Then I could feel the line rising and knew the bass was coming to the surface.

"Dad!"

It thrashed the water, too big to jump free, and wallowed half-submerged, shaking its head, throwing spray that sounded like bucket-water flung in the darkness. The bass dove and I knew I would lose it. It would wrap around thickets of weeds and break the line.

"Dad! Take the rod! It's going for the weeds!"

"You're doing fine. Keep the rod high."

"I don't want to lose it! You bring it in!"

"You hooked it, you can land it or lose it yourself."

"Dad!"

"Just let him fight, let him wear himself out."

I t's strange that I don't recall other bass caught those nights. I know there were many, because my father still talks about them, but for me the nights have all blended into that one night, and all the other fish have been forgotten. There is a photograph enlarged and framed in my parents' house of my brother and me hoisting the five-pound largemouth between us, my brother there because we woke him when we returned with the fish and he wanted to share the glory. I remember the sudden flash of the camera, and the spot of brilliance that blinded me for minutes afterward, and my mother laughing and saying it was the biggest bass she had ever seen, though I knew even then that it wasn't. I remember too the relief that had flooded over me when the large, black creature in the water was finally swept into my father's landing net and swung into the boat where it thumped against the aluminum two, three times, then was still. And I remember my father switching on the flashlight and shining it on the fish, seeing it illuminated suddenly, sheening with water, its mouth clamped down, even in defeat, on the little frog-colored lure.

By most standards it was not a trophy bass, but when you considered those five pounds in relation to my seventy-five pounds the fish gained significance. My father would have needed to catch one weighing nearly fifteen pounds to equal the achievement.

"It's fat as a piglet," he said when he had it in the net, but to me it looked bigger yet, fat as a sow. I could not imagine a larger bass living in our lake. To this day I have not caught one that can match it.

ENCOUNTER IN
THE CATTAILS

When I was ten years old and my brother eight, our father gave us his old Boy Scout pocket-knife and a military compass and seemed to suggest it was time we struck out on our own. We lived on Silver Lake then, in our first house on the water, on a point jutting into the neck of a large, gourd-shaped bay surrounded by marshes at the far end and high ground and cottages on the other. For years my brother and I had taken short expeditions down the shore of the bay, as far from home as we could go in an hour or two. It was a little frightening to go farther: Older neighbor children told stories of quicksand pits among the cattail marshes; they said kids had been sucked down so quickly nothing was left but their crabbed hands raised in agony above the sand.

But that summer, made bold by our new freedom, Rick and I began wandering farther and farther from home. On the shore of the bay where there were no cottages, we waded among the cattails looking for such treasures as fishermen's lures and tennis balls, newly hatched snapping turtles the size of half-dollars, dense schools of silver shiners that panicked and leaped from the water when we cornered them in the shallows. To our disappointment, we found no quicksand.

One day, equipped with the knife and compass, a war-surplus canteen, a book of matches (our mother didn't know), and a woefully tattered copy of *The Golden Nature Guide to the Most Familiar American Birds*, we set out to circle the entire bay. The bird book was an essential part of our equipment that summer. Already Rick and I had spotted and identified such exotics as rose-breasted grosbeaks, scarlet tanagers, and cedar waxwings. We had passed hours watching a Baltimore oriole sway in its sack-lunch nest high in the silver maple at the end of our driveway, and had seen male cardinals bright as drops of blood in the cedars in our yard. Now we were on the lookout for something different, any bird we could identify only with the aid of the guidebook.

At the marsh, red-winged blackbirds flitted to the tops of the cattails, bending them with their weight, winging away with blinking flashes of scarlet. It was one of those timeless summer days, pure with blue sky and sun, the temperature perfect for cutoffs and T-shirts. Washed up in the shallows were occasional dead fish, sun-faded soda cans, and rubber balls. Farther along we found, of all things, a ripe yellow grapefruit. It seemed proof of our independence, evidence that we could support ourselves on these forays. We peeled it and halved it, then ate it in segments like an orange.

As we ate I scanned the lake. It was a weekday and the bay was deserted. In the evening, after our father returned home from calling on businesses and convincing them they had need for a new device called a Thermo-Fax Copier, we would probably go out in the boat to troll over the weed beds for pike. If the fishing was good we would stay on the water until dark, then drift along the shoreline casting into the night for largemouth bass.

The lake was blue, ruffled by the wind. Low waves came over our knees and set the shore weeds in motion. I turned and peered through the waving fronds of the marsh grasses. Something moved among the cattails. I strained to see through the stalks and grasses and saw it again: a twitch, a too-sudden movement. Then, like those picture riddles in which you search among familiar objects to find something out of place, a strange bird took shape.

I knew what it was immediately: an American bittern. It was illustrated on page 26 of the Golden Guide, preceded in sequence by the great blue heron, the green heron, and the stately black-crowned night heron. It seemed so out of place in such company that I had always felt sorry for it. The illustration and description portrayed it as short, squat, humpbacked, a dull and colorless creature that preferred solitude and rarely ventured outside the marshes where it lived. Little wonder, I thought. It was absolutely homely, made all wrong—too paunchy and low-slung, with not enough wing or leg to support its girth, and with a peculiar skulking way of holding its head forward and low beneath the unfortunate hump—a Peter Lorre of the bird world.

As Rick and I watched, the bittern transformed itself, stretching and rising dramatically into a new, elongated shape. Made somehow thin, almost elegant, it began to sway, moving in time with the wind and the cattails. One eye, the entire time, remained on us. We stayed frozen, eyes locked, all waiting for the others to do something.

Our father has always been a passable mimic of bird songs. He can call crows and ducks through his cupped hands, can whistle melodically and be answered by songbirds in trees beyond our yard. In this situation his response would have been to call like a bittern to see what would happen. I knew the bird was sometimes known as a "thunder pumper" or "stake driver," in reference to its call, which was supposed to be an unusual "pumping" sound, though I was unsure what that meant. If it was a sound like the old hand pump in the backyard of our grandparents' farm, then it was rhythmic and rasping, in need of oil, followed by rumbling gulps of water deep in the earth. I tried my best to approximate the sound, gurgling and thrusting air from far down in my throat. Rick joined me. We tried so hard that we closed our eyes to concentrate and attempted by willpower alone to be solitary, odd-looking birds in rueful need of fellowship.

When we opened our eyes, it was gone. We searched carefully through the stalks of cattails, but could see nothing out of place.

It seemed an appropriate way to end the encounter. We marked page 26 of the guidebook with a ballpoint pen, and checked off the name in the index.

Half the bay stretched ahead of us. We continued along the shore, dreaming of danger and treasures, practicing bird songs, testing the boundaries of our world.

A LEGENDARY FISH

During the four years we lived on Silver Lake my father often talked about moving a few miles west to Long Lake, the largest lake in our lake-strewn county, and one that had for decades been famous for its northern pike. Long Lake was big and sprawling, spattered with islands and points and deep, reaching bays large enough to be small lakes themselves, and much of it was ideal habitat for pike. Fishermen we met on Silver Lake or at bait shops talked about the huge northerns cruising the bays and drop-offs of Long Lake, hiding among the weed beds, regularly destroying the fishing tackle of summer anglers who didn't know what they were getting into when they dared cast into the lake.

But during the time my father dreamed of moving there,

Long Lake was in decline. For years, in the winter after the tourists left, the locals had taken their revenge in spearing shanties. Sometimes the north end looked like a miniature city, the shanties trailing delicate wisps of stove smoke, the cars parked among them on the ice, the tracks worn to narrow streets through the snow from shore. On a good day—and at first there were many good days—anyone with a sure hand could spear a limit of five pike that averaged ten pounds each, and could, with luck, go home with one that weighed twenty or twenty-five pounds. The lake's reputation spread. It began to attract larger crowds until even in winter the tourists were coming, renting cabins that were traditionally shuttered after Labor Day. And then the big pike disappeared.

We came too late to the lake. The first summer after we moved from Silver Lake, when I was nine, I spent much of every day casting oversize spoons from the end of the dock in front of our new house. A neighbor told me, with a suggestion of menace, that he had caught many large pike from that same dock. "There's drowned logs out there," he said. "Those pike like to lay beside them. Keep casting and sooner or later . . ."

I believed him. I cast in early morning and late evening, losing lures to snags if I let them settle too long after the cast, sometimes growing bored and casting straight up into the sky, watching the lure pause at its apex, then descend, accelerating until it hurtled into the water without splashing, like a high diver. Occasionally I hooked smallmouth bass a foot or fourteen inches long. But I caught no pike.

Some of our neighbors claimed ten years of low water had blocked the channel to Ruth Lake, a shallow, weed-clogged pond adjacent to Long Lake that provided an important spawning habitat for the main lake's pike. Others blamed the Michigan Department of Natural Resources for planting walleyes and brown trout, species not native to the lake. A few fishermen admitted they might have killed too many big pike.

My father, brother, and I learned the secrets of the lake gradually. We fished it year-round, trolling and casting in the summer, setting tip-ups baited with shiners and small suckers in the winter. We caught bass and walleyes and sometimes oddly shaped pike of two or three pounds—pike with too-large heads and stunted, malformed bodies—but we caught nothing to compete with the fish in the tales our neighbors told. Most of the people who talked about the lake's lost glory no longer fished it. In the summers we shared the water with water-skiers and pleasure boaters. In the winters we had it mostly to ourselves.

I was more stubborn than informed. Refusing to believe that trophy northerns, once present in the lake, would not be present forever, I hoarded stories of large fish that had been hooked and lost, as if each was evidence the lake was returning to its former greatness. One neighbor, a man with the lined, leathery face of someone who has spent much time outdoors, showed me the dozen dried heads of northern pike—each large enough to hold a softball in its mouth—nailed to the trunks of trees in his yard, and described how he caught each of them by casting ten-inch suckers on bobbers off the end of his dock. He caught pike up to twenty pounds, he said, and once or twice had hooked fish so big he could not stop them as they ran and lost them finally when they stripped all the line from his reel. Our first winter on the lake my father saw such a fish while he sat in our spearing shanty—a pike so big it filled the hole though it was ten feet below the ice when it passed through, a pike so scarred and mean-looking it reminded Dad of a street fighter, arrogant and battle-wise and accustomed to being feared. Those stories sustained me through some of the longest, least productive fishing days I have ever known.

Winter was the one season when I could fish the deep water of the lake without my parents' company. I was not interested in panfish, so never bothered with the dainty ice rods and teardrop jigs other anglers used for perch and blue-gills. I was after big game, and fished exclusively with tip-ups and minnows. A tip-up is among the simplest of fishing tools. There are many styles, but the ones I used were made of a spool of line attached to a wooden shaft with another piece of wood as a crosspiece. The crosspiece held the tip-up in place on the ice, while the spool was submerged in the water and kept from turning by the pressure of a loop of wire. If a fish took the bait—a minnow suspended on the line beneath the spool—it tripped the wire, causing it to spring upright and wave a small red flag at its tip. The spool turned freely as the fish ran with the bait, and an angler would take up the line and pull the fish in hand over hand. Once set, a tip-up had the advantage of working whether supervised or not, allowing me to take refuge in the house if I was cold. From there, with the fireplace beating warmly at my back, I could watch for tripped flags from the picture window.

Our second year on the lake I set a pair of tip-ups every day during Christmas vacation and caught nothing. I fished every Saturday and Sunday in January and still caught nothing. By February the snow was so deep the ice sank beneath it, turning the surface to slush that sucked at my boots and left the bottoms of my trousers soaked and frozen. Then it froze into twenty inches of bad ice and more snow came, sank the ice again, and added another ten inches of bad ice.

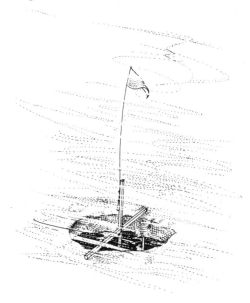

I spudded two holes in front of our house, in the area of the sunken logs, and decided to fish there the remainder of the winter.

I rose early one Sunday morning, while my parents slept, and set my lines in a snowstorm. The wind had begun the night before, blowing down from the north across the open lake, lifting snow in huge, swirling devils that built drifts across the fronts of the lakeside houses. Snow squalls raced over the ice, obliterating entire islands. When they swept over me I turned my back and huddled into my parka, the snow slashing my face, my fingers aching from reaching bare-handed into the bait bucket. I blocked the tip-ups in place with chunks of ice, careful to set them so the wind would not trip the flags, then hurried back to the house to wait.

Later that morning, watching with binoculars from the living room window, I could see the small flags waving frantically, like distress signals. "Wind flags," I thought. I waded through the snow to the lake and gathered the bucket of minnows, the ice scoop, and my father's ancient gaff. I walked backward, against the wind, and thought of things other than fishing.

The first spool, submerged in the water beneath the ice, was empty of line. It ran at an angle under the ice, toward the other tip-up. Both flags were up and I guessed that a fish had snared the second line while it ran with the bait. I threw down my mittens, grasped the line, and hauled back hard to set the hook.

The line stretched in resistance against a heavy weight, but I gained nothing. I could feel the line rubbing across obstructions, giving slightly, and beyond it the muted struggle of something alive. I pulled as hard as I dared and gained a yard, then another. Gradually the line gathered in loose coils on the snow. Only occasionally did I feel the slow tugging of a fish, like a dog shaking a heavy boot.

I remembered the stories I had heard, of massive pike seen through shanty holes, of fish that had stripped line and left rods and tip-ups shattered. Someone had hooked a twenty-five-pound northern on a tip-up and fought it for thirty minutes before he realized it would not fit through the small hole he had cut in the ice. He landed it finally after holding the line in one hand and using the other to enlarge the hole with his spud. Sometimes we heard about bass and walleyes found with deep, narrow lacerations across their backs—wounds you would expect to find on minnows or panfish, not adult fish weighing two or three pounds. Or we would hear a panfisherman lament that a bluegill he had been bringing to the surface was stripped from him, grabbed by something unseen and huge.

I gained line a foot at a time, accumulating coils of frozen line on the ice. The useless hook and sinker from my second tip-up came into the hole, tangled around the taut line, and I cut them free with my pocketknife. I could feel the distant fish, closer now, but there was still a lot of line out. My tip-ups were equipped for big fish, spooled with a hundred yards of twenty-pound-test braided Dacron line and a five-foot length of equally strong monofilament leader. Only a big fish could put so much strain on line that strong.

The swivel attaching the line to the monofilament leader appeared. Bits of decomposing leaves and mud swirled in the water. The stubborn, muted tugging of the struggling fish was close now, less than five feet away. I was aware that I stood alone on the lake, a small, red-hooded figure lost in a white landscape.

Until then I had imagined I could land the fish, even hoped that it was nothing more than a reasonably large northern tangled in ten pounds of debris. But my position was less certain than that. I was never in control at all. The head-shaking became more definite now and more powerful. The line began pulling through my hands. It lifted from the snow, ran between my fingers, and disappeared back into the lake. I slowed the run as much as I could, tightening until I feared the line would break, then releasing another five, ten, fifteen yards. The fish moved off steadily, without panic. It had allowed itself to be led nearly to the hole, but when it tired of the game it simply turned toward deep water and swam away.

There was nothing I could do. I clung as tightly to the line as possible. But I could not stop the fish. It swam off in a sustained, powerful, unstoppable run until it took back all the line, and the tip-up I had thrown out of the way on the ice plowed through the snow toward the hole. The empty spool entered the water and I held it back with both hands. The line strained tighter, too tight, then gave way finally far away, at the junction of the line and leader.

My fingers began to hurt later, at home, after they were pulled from the mittens and placed under running water in the sink. The storm swirling silently beyond the windows seemed far away and harmless. My mother was angry that I had gone out in such weather. She and my father had been asleep the entire time, and I knew they felt negligent in not being there to help. At least I knew that later. Then, at the sink, I knew nothing. I talked on and on, my nose running freely, my cheeks and ears flaming in the sudden warmth of the kitchen. My father stopped me finally, his hands firm on my shoulders, and told me to slow down, to tell them again in words they could understand exactly what had happened.

THE QUICKNESS
OF TROUT

I became at a very early age
something of a trout snob. That's a common enough tendency
among adults but unusual for a boy of ten or twelve, especially one who fished with worms and bobbers and a budget
spin-casting outfit. Though I was ready to testify that of all
the earth's creatures trout were the loveliest and the most
precious—the finned equivalent of blue diamonds and uni-
corns—I had a problem: I had never caught a trout; I had
never (this was difficult to admit) even seen a trout.

Years later, in college in Louisville, Kentucky, hundreds
of miles from the nearest trout stream and so unhappy about
it that I searched doggedly through my reading for any mention, no matter how oblique, of running water and speckled
fish, I would see my interest in trout defined in a vitriolic

essay titled "The Novel," by the English novelist D. H. Lawrence. In that essay Lawrence describes a quality called "quickness" found in certain objects and creatures. A being with quickness, he explains, is more than merely lifelike, it is filled with a "god-flame" that elevates it above the ordinary. It possesses "a certain weird relationship between that which is quick and . . . all the rest of things. It seems to consist in an odd sort of fluid, changing, grotesque or beautiful relatedness." With imagery sure to catch an angler's eye, Lawrence went on to say that "the relatedness and interrelatedness of all things flows and changes and trembles like a stream, and like a fish in the stream the characters in the novel swim and drift and float and turn belly-up when they're dead."

Had Lawrence been a fisherman, it is likely he would have specified his fish as trout, and particularly the small native brook trout of eastern North America. Brown trout, rainbow trout, cutthroat trout, golden trout, and all other trout possess qualities of quickness, but I'm convinced brook trout possess the most quickness of all. Never mind that they do not grow as large as brown trout or as vigorous as rainbow trout. They are alive, vibrant, rare creatures of extraordinary vitality and innocence: quick.

Long before I had heard of D. H. Lawrence, my fascination with trout was superficial, a matter of color. I knew the colors of trout best from Winslow Homer prints clipped from sporting magazines and thumbtacked to my walls. Brook trout, like beach stones, cardinals, ruby-throated hummingbirds, violets, autumn leaves, and rainbows, were fascinating because they were charged with brilliance. In contrast to the earth browns and forest greens of the northern Michigan landscape I was familiar with, a creature spotted in vermilion and orange became priceless.

We lived in country famous for its trout streams. Only a few miles from our house was the Boardman River, with a reputation for big brown trout in the lower river and a healthy population of naturally reproducing brook trout in the upper river. Fifty miles beyond it was the Au Sable, the best-known trout river in the Midwest, the birthplace of the conservation organization Trout Unlimited, and home to untold fortunes in brook, brown, and rainbow trout. Between those streams, draining the small valleys of our hilly countryside, were dozens, even hundreds, of rivers and streams, most of them inhabited by brook trout.

Yet, my home was in the center of a lake-rich township where the only streams were mud-bottomed canals connecting warm-water lakes. In them were found, not trout, but bluegill, perch, bass, and pike—crude and loutish creatures by comparison. My father had little interest in small creeks or tiny brook trout. He would take me trolling or casting for bass and pike in the lake, but he saw no point in driving to the Boardman or Au Sable rivers. It was left for me to explore the few streams within reach by bicycle, and to pursue on my own every rumor of hidden trout lairs.

Almost everything I knew about trout fishing I had learned from outdoor magazines, which I devoured greedily, and from watching Curt Gowdy on television's "American Sportsman." I came to realize that advanced trout snobs fished only with fly rods and dry flies, but my early experience flailing my father's enormous and battered fiberglass fly rod with its heavy automatic reel had been so disheartening that I decided—wisely, I think—to first master the less subtle arts of bait fishing and spin fishing. There would be plenty of time later for fly rods. In the meantime, the top priority was to actually catch a trout.

I was not alone in my ambition. My best friend, Del Houghton, a neighborhood kid with intense passions for baseball, fishing, and food, shared my assessment of the virtues of trout. Del was large for his age, gentle, patient, with a bizarre sense of humor, and could perform a repertoire of character roles, including a remarkably deft imitation of Jonathan Winters. He ate enormously, cared deeply about money, and had learned to make a symphony of sounds with an open palm in the pit of his arm.

Each April, as the opening day of trout season approached, Del and I prepared for the event with the zeal of true trout fanatics. We equipped ourselves with medicine bottles filled with new hooks and split shot, and collected worms and crickets from beneath the wet, flattened leaves behind our parents' woodpiles. Early on the Saturday of each opening day we launched expeditions by bicycle to a succession of sluggish, weed-lined sloughs and channels we were certain harbored overlooked populations of brook trout. We caught only chubs and rock bass, but were never discouraged. Even while riding home fishless we were already planning other, more ambitious outings.

One May, near the end of the school year, we learned of a fantastic trout pond in our neighborhood, a pond so thoroughly hidden that even people who had lived near it all their lives did not know it was there. The information came from a younger boy on the school bus who, overhearing us talking about fishing and hoping to win favor, turned around in his seat to describe in detail where we could find trout hidden in a swamp on his grandfather's property.

We pressed for details. The pond was definitely inhabited by trout, he said. Brook trout? Brown trout? He didn't know, he couldn't tell one trout from another, but he thought they were brook trout. They had spots. Colored spots that could belong only to trout. He had seen them. He had caught them. Trout. We made him draw us a map.

We left Del's house at dawn that Saturday, in the middle of mosquito season, our rods strapped to the handlebars of our bikes, canteens and canvas creels slung from our shoulders. We pumped our bikes up the discouraging hills on Long Lake Road, coasted on the downslopes. In our pockets we carried compasses, pocketknives, matches, and Juicy Fruit.

The pond was at the center of a section of lowlands and swamps surrounded by failed farms and struggling Christmas-tree plantations. There was, of course, no easy way to reach it. We stashed our bikes in the underbrush at the side of the road and pushed into the dark, fetid world of the swamp.

Mosquitoes converged on us with maddening certainty. We were prepared with our pre-ozone-worry aerosols of repellent. But Del's can had leaked dry, and the nozzle on mine had broken off and been lost. Fighting panic, clawing at exposed skin, we transferred Del's nozzle to my can and sprayed wildly about us, like the happy lady in the Pine-Sol commercials.

We never became actually lost. The swamp was sectioned into a precise square by four gravel roads. Each time we came to a road we simply reversed directions, re-dosed ourselves with repellent, took another reading with our compasses (mine did not agree with Del's), and set off again for the center of the swamp. Every mosquito bite, every branch slapping our faces, every lurching step through clinging brambles enhanced our determination. It made the journey eventful and separated us from the legions of less committed anglers. By the time we discovered the pond, glittering through a tangle of cedars and tag alders, we were stoked to explode in anticipation.

The pond was smaller than we expected, not much larger than a baseball infield, and could be reached only by climbing over ancient fallen trees around its edges. Hidden as it was, isolated by swamps and inconvenience, it seemed never to have been fished. It seemed to be trembling with quickness.

We maneuvered over the tangled logs until we reached open sunlight at the edge of the water. If we had slipped from the logs we balanced on we would have fallen into bottomless muck. Gray skeletons of trees stood upright around the shore, and lily pads grew in the shallows. Damsel flies hovered delicately. A trio of turtles dropped, in sequence, off a silvered log.

Carefully, attending to each detail, we rigged our rods with hooks and bobbers, baiting with small, lively leaf worms. Del chanted: "Trout, trout, trout." The word alone, whispered like a mantra, was enough to thrill us.

The summer before, at the end of the Little League season, Del had voted for me to be the team's most valuable player, as a best friend should, while I, in a failure of nerve, had voted for myself. It was a betrayal that had haunted me all winter, and now I was determined to make up for it. I looked out over the glittering surface of our Shangri-la, the water I knew was infested with brook trout of uncommon size and enthusiasm, trout that would leap all over one another in their rush to reach our bait, and with a magnanimous gesture said to Del, "You go first."

His bobber and bait swung over the pond like a gaucho's bola, landing in the open water beyond the fringe of lily pads. Even before the rings from the cast disappeared the bobber trembled, transmitting urgent ripples, then plunged beneath the surface. Del heaved back, bending his rod deeply, shouting in triumph. A fish skittered to the surface and slid toward us: a bluegill, perhaps four inches long.

I cast and immediately hooked an identical bluegill.

Del baited again and cast and caught another.

To snobs like us the disappointment was cutting. Yet, when we held the tiny fish in our palms, careful to fold the spines back so they would not pierce our skin, they were extraordinary. In the sunlight, high and beaming from the open sky, the tiny flanks erupted with the faintest blues and greens and oranges, all suffused with subtle variations of the spectrum.

And yes, there were spots. Del noticed first. They were not the prominent features, but if you looked closely you saw them: small and roundish and stippled with an almost troutlike brilliance.

THE
CHRISTMAS GIFT

There was a year when Tony's mother forgot all about Christmas. None of us was surprised, and nobody blamed her. She had other things on her mind.

Tony and I lived a few houses apart on Long Lake and for years had spent many of our spare hours together, exploring the lakes and woods near home. We knew each other like brothers. He was fourteen that winter, skinny and so tall he was in the habit already of stooping at doorways. His father had died in August, after a long illness, and Tony had decided he was responsible for two little brothers who had to be kept away from matches and knives, and for a thirteen-year-old sister who was nearly as tall as Tony and possessed not a trace of respect for his authority. He had decided also that it was his duty to cheer his mother for the holidays and that a dinner of baked grouse and pike fillets would distract her from her troubles. I came from a turkey and ham family myself, and was a stickler for tradition, but I went along with Tony's plan because he was my friend.

In those days we sometimes hunted grouse with my dog, Lady, a fat-as-a-sausage beagle who in her prime had been known to climb trees after squirrels and was the only beagle I have ever heard of that would point birds. She had grown up with a pair of my father's Brittany spaniels and had learned to lock into a rigid, trembling, belly-to-the-ground point whenever she scented a game bird. You could trust Lady's points, but she was easily distracted by rabbits, squirrels, and deer. You also had to watch her around raccoons, porcupines, and skunks.

Tony and I had one gun between us, a sleek and ancient single-shot twelve-gauge that kicked like a howitzer and had been presented to me with formal solemnity on my twelfth birthday. It had been my father's first gun, presented to him by my grandfather, and it was understood that I would eventually pass it on to my own son or daughter. It was my most treasured possession, a man's gun, and I was more proud of it than anything I owned. The day after I received it, my father had taken me to his duck blind at the Mud Lake Flooding, where I promptly dropped a drake mallard that rocketed past at sixty yards. It was the only bird I ever got with that gun.

Over the years, Tony and I shot at a lot of grouse with my shotgun, but we never killed one. They were too fast and evasive for us. We would watch them thunder away, not a feather ruffled, and shake our heads and laugh. If it had been Tony's turn to shoot, he would hold the gun up and admire it. "This is a sweet shotgun," he would say. I agreed. "You take good care of this baby," he said. I would. I promised. But more often than not it was he, not I, who cleaned it at the end of a day of hunting.

Our effort to shoot a grouse for Christmas nearly failed because the snow was so deep that poor Lady could not keep up with us. She was forced to practically tunnel through the woods and kept going off in random directions, whining in frustration, and snorting up little spouts of snow. She finally flushed a grouse from dense hemlocks, but it flew off on the far side of the trees and all Tony and I saw of it was the trail of sifting snowfall as it passed through a stand of evergreens. We hunted three or four days without seeing another bird, until, unexpectedly, with Lady miles away, we almost stepped on one that was roosting in the snow. It blew up from the loose fluff, throwing snow like we'd stepped on a land mine. If I had been carrying the gun I would have been too startled to even think of wasting a shell. But Tony swung on the bird, fired, and it tumbled dead into the snow. We could not have been more surprised. We dressed it and took it home to store in my parents' freezer.

Tony had already decided the only way to get a northern pike large enough to feed his entire family was to spear it. I had little hope for success. Long Lake's pike population had continued to decline and the few survivors were battle-wizened and cautious. Besides, neither Tony nor I had any experience throwing spears at fish. It was a legal and time-honored practice, but my father frowned on it, proclaiming it underhanded and archaic, a sanctioned form of cheating that had spoiled fishing in Long Lake. Tony's father had at one time been enthused enough to build a shanty and equip it with a stove and spear, but an ice shanty requires almost daily maintenance. If you did not frequently jack up the corners and support them with blocks of wood, the entire structure sank gradually into the ice until the only way to get it off the lake was to chain-saw the freestanding portion, leaving the floor behind. Tony's father had been a long-distance trucker, home too seldom to give proper attention to the shanty. Eventually he had pulled it to shore and left it there, perched on cement blocks beneath the birches.

The day before Christmas Tony and I spent the morning digging the shanty out of the snow and dragging it with his toboggan onto the lake. So much snow had fallen that the ice was sinking, forcing water to the surface and forming slush.

We spudded a three-by-three-foot hole in the ice and horsed the shanty into position over it. Once it was in place, and the hole scooped clear, we banked up snow around the shanty to keep light from seeping inside. We ignited the stove. When we closed the door we were enveloped in darkness.

As our eyes adjusted we looked down the hole into an unexpected world. Lit green like an aquarium, quiet as the inside of the earth, it was a world you wouldn't know even existed if all you saw of a lake in winter was the featureless snow that covered it. On the bottom, ten feet down, rested wisps of pikeweed and skeletal maple leaves. On the surface of the lake everything was white and frozen to stillness. Down below was color and movement and life.

Tony picked up his father's spear and removed the block of wood that protected its six sharp tines. The shaft measured five feet long, and was weighted at the bottom with two pounds of lead. An eyelet at the other end was attached to a coil of cord.

We used a wooden decoy weighted with a lead core and shaped like an eight-inch, red-and-white sucker. Tony tied it to a spool of braided line and lowered it into the water. He jigged it and it swam in circles, rising and falling like a merry-go-round horse. If he stopped jigging, the decoy rested dead and wooden in the water. If he jerked it, it soared like a startled bird.

The interior of the shanty warmed and we took off our jackets. I turned to hang mine on the wall and bumped the spear, knocking it hurtling in a stream of bubbles to the bottom. When the water cleared the spear rested at an odd angle in the muck. Tony pulled it to the surface, bringing up a trail of leaf parts and mud. Then he sent the spear into the water again—not throwing it so much as pushing it off, letting the weight do the work. It shot straight down and stuck in the bottom. I took a turn, aiming at a length of weed I could imagine was a fish. Tony balanced the spear again on the edge of the hole and we settled down to wait.

Sitting there in the warm, dark shanty, I started thinking about Christmas. Like Tony, I was fourteen that year, and though I no longer approached the holiday with the same expectations I had as a child, I was reluctant to give them up. For months I'd been dropping hints about a gasoline-powered airplane. I knew it was not a sensible gift because it required a broad expanse of concrete or asphalt for take-offs and landings, and there was no such place for ten miles in any direction of our house. But I was child enough still to want a child's toy. I wanted the old excitement.

"Tony," I said, "what do you want for Christmas?"

He turned slowly, his mind elsewhere. His face was lit from below with eerie light. "I don't know," he said. "Nothing much."

"Nothing much? Come on."

"Some school clothes. Maybe a hunting knife."

I said nothing about the airplane.

I took a long turn with the decoy. After awhile my arm moved independently of me. The decoy below vaulted and sailed, and seemed to have no connection to my arm. I started getting restless. I wondered why Tony was not content to just eat store-bought turkey like everyone else.

I handed the decoy line back to him and stood to put on my coat.

"I'm going for a walk," I said.

Outside, I stomped a circle in the slush and waited for it to freeze so I would have a dry place to stand. The sun was low on the hilltops, the day fading down to pale blue and the cold night air descending. A few other shanties were scattered across our end of the lake, but they sat unused and frozen-looking. I imagined my parents at home, preparing for our traditional Christmas celebration. I thought of Tony's mother, then of his father. I had preferred death when it was an abstract concept. That summer it had struck too close to home and I did not know what to think. Tony and I never talked about it, not once. I convinced myself he preferred it that way.

Then Tony shouted. I spun and looked at the shanty. There was a clatter inside and the shanty seemed to rock and tremble, like a cartoon rocket about to launch. The door burst open and Tony tumbled out, his spear at waist level impaled through a gyrating northern pike. He could hardly hold it up.

Ten pounds, I thought in disbelief. Fifteen pounds. Tony threw it down on the ice and danced in triumph around it.

It was not fifteen pounds. More like ten. Eight, to be honest. But it was large enough for Christmas dinner. Tony's grin was so broad I thought his face would cramp. He told me what had happened, how the fish had appeared suddenly, without warning. One moment there was nothing, the next there was a northern pike, the largest he had ever seen, hovering in the center of the hole. It had focused intently on the decoy, its fins waving to keep it in position. Tony had pushed the spear off firmly, the way we had practiced.

We walked to shore, stepping in the plugged and frozen footprints we had made coming out. Tony waited while I ran up the hill and took the wrapped grouse from my parents' freezer. Then we walked together to his house, like wise men bearing gifts.

His mother sat alone in the kitchen, dressed in a sweatshirt and jeans, her hair pulled back and pinned so tight it stretched the skin taut on her face. The house was dark, the table empty. No food cooked merrily on the stove. I realized for the first time what Tony had been so determined to do, and it made me ashamed for not taking his efforts more seriously. I was ashamed, too, because my family was so stable and complete, our Christmas so abundant that the bounty overflowed outdoors. There were wreaths on our doors and an electric Santa on the roof and a two-string coil of blinking blue lights around the spruce beside the driveway. Inside were Christmas music, a crackling fire, dishes heaped with nuts and the chocolate candies my mother made every year. Our Christmas tree was large and full, lit as bright as the night sky, with an enormous silver star on top. I was ashamed and grateful and guilty all at once. Tony and his sister had set up a tree, but it was skinny and sparse, with a few tinny ornaments and a scattering of tinsel. I realized then, with the kind of sudden, irrefutable insight kids are prone to, that Tony's family could not stay here much longer, that the house would be sold, that this would be the last Christmas we would spend as neighbors.

It took her a few moments to notice us, but when she saw what we were offering she smiled. She motioned for us to put the fish and grouse in the sink, then pulled Tony into her arms in a hug. His sister and brothers appeared. Everyone was smiling. That evening they would have the goofiest Christmas meal of their lives and it would be a turning point they would always remember—not the first Christmas without their father, but the Christmas Tony brought home pike and grouse for dinner.

It was nearly dark. I headed home, following the deep trail Tony and I kept open all winter between our houses, and walked in on my mother's usual Christmas Eve feast. My grandparents were there, and uncles and aunts, and all my cousins. There was venison, sliced thin and served with gravy, as a side course to the turkey. We had mashed potatoes, stuffing, sweet potatoes with melted marshmallows, cranberry sauce, two or three kinds of pie, and ice cream. I watched my father as if I had never seen him: A big man at the head of the table, his sleeves rolled up, laughing at someone's joke while he used a carving knife and fork to slice the turkey into thick white slabs. I was never so grateful to have him home.

In the morning we opened presents and to my surprise I was handed, not a gasoline-powered airplane, but a mysterious, long, heavy package. I tore into it with fear and disbelief. Inside was a new pump-action twenty-gauge shotgun. It was the exact gun I had been coveting in catalogs for years. I had always been so sure it was beyond any possibility of possession that I had never dared mention it to my father.

I was stunned. My parents sat close together, their eyes bright, watching my reaction. I could not believe they would buy me such a gift. Their generosity humbled me. I wanted to emulate it.

After breakfast I cleaned and oiled my old twelve-gauge and replaced it inside its leather case. I wrapped it in Christmas paper.

My father watched. "What about shells?" he asked. He helped wrap two boxes. They made heavy, satisfying packages in my jacket pockets.

Outside it was cold, the morning air harsh, the snow crunching underfoot like Styrofoam. Tony came to his door wearing a new sweater over his pajamas. Behind him his brothers stood five feet from one another, screaming into a pair of walkie-talkies. Tony grinned at the commotion and stepped aside to invite me in, but I stood my ground, hands behind my back, breath hanging in the cold air.

I'll never forget his eyes, the way they grew wider and wider as I held the bright package out to him.

IN THE
BUFFALO FIELDS

ollowing the long descending sweep of highway into the city, a car at night would send its headlights like a search beacon across the buffalo fields. Late-night motorists were often startled to wakefulness at the sight of the great, shaggy, stupid creatures standing in clusters near the fence, an approximate vision of the Big Horn Valley before Custer, a mirage from early American plains life. But this was caricature, history misplaced, a piece of the continent's lost memory made manifest and lifted from Wyoming or Montana or North Dakota and set in a cow pasture in northern Michigan. It was fenced with barbed wire six feet high and labeled with a large, proud sign next to the highway that read: "Oleson's Buffalo Herd—Largest East of the Mississippi."

I hated that sign. In the mornings, riding past in the crowded school bus, it reminded me that the fields were not the entrance to wild, unfettered range country. The buffalo were raised for slaughter, their loins ground into burgers and barbecue sandwiches sold to tourists. I did my best to ignore that, choosing to remember instead that the animals on occasion staged minor rampages, breaking down sections of fence to invade the right-of-way of the highway, creating a sensation in the parking lot of the mobile-home dealership across the road.

Midway across the buffalo fields, strung through a dense grove of cedar trees, was a series of small ponds where rainbow trout were raised for consumption, their fillets appearing each week beside the buffalo steaks in the display counters of Oleson's two grocery stores. The ponds were fed by a small, lively trout stream marked on maps as Asylum Creek —named for the old state-owned hospital it skirted farther downstream—but known to everyone in Traverse City as Kid's Creek. It originated in a swamp at the back of Oleson's property, meandered through the open fields of the buffalo farm to the trout ponds, and exited through a culvert at the edge of the highway. From there to its junction with the Boardman River two miles downstream, the creek supported trout and, in an unwritten edict, was fished only by the children of our community. In spring and fall, steelhead entered the stream and could sometimes be caught with spinners or spawn bags, or, if you were skilled enough, with bare hands. During the summer we fished the deep pools and undercut banks where the creek flowed through the meadows above the state hospital, catching wild brookies and brown trout and occasional rainbows that had escaped downstream from Oleson's ponds.

When my friends and I were old enough to drive, we exercised our new mobility by seeking out new streams and lakes to fish. Doug, Russ, Wes, and I would load our tackle in the trunk of Doug's Torino, when it was running, or borrow my father's Buick Wildcat convertible, when he was in a generous mood, and spend our free hours exploring the far reaches of our county. Before returning home I was always careful to pull away the field grass and stray branches that caught on the undercarriage of my father's Buick during our explorations. If he had seen the places we took his car I would have been riding bikes and school buses for years to come.

For Christmas that year my parents had given me a South Bend fiberglass fly rod and matching Finalist reel and I had spent the winter tying clumsy flies and casting them on the ice of the lake, trying to drop them into a small area of water that remained open in the channel between Long Lake and Mickey Lake. For years before that I occasionally cast my father's fly rod off the end of our dock and caught bluegills and small bass, but I was impatient with those unselective bumpkins—they would strike a fragment of cork as readily as a Quill Gordon dry fly. I wanted to catch trout with my new fly rod. By the time the season opened at the end of April I had whipped myself to a frenzy.

One afternoon in early May my father and I loaded our equipment in the trunk of the car and drove to the Boardman River. Dad was not a trout fisherman. His passions were for pike, bass, and walleyes from inland lakes, and he was most at ease in a rowboat, slinging bass plugs toward the lily pads, or trolling Flatfish and Daredevls while the old outboard motor coughed and sputtered but never stalled, idling so slowly you could see the propeller turning. On a trout stream he seemed clumsy and poorly equipped. His old rod and automatic fly reel were too large for the small river, and unstylish. He, who was so confident with spinning tackle on lakes, seemed uncertain of himself and tentative in a narrow stream with quick current. After tangling a few backcasts in the trees and losing some dollar flies, he stomped off to listen to a baseball game on the car radio.

I tangled in the trees as well, but managed every third or fourth cast to lay my leader and fly on the water in what I guessed was a proper manner. The sensation was exhilarating. It was like accidentally striking a perfect chord while pounding on the piano, or like driving a golf ball on a straight, true arc down the fairway after hours of uncontrolled slices and hooks. Each time the leader straightened in the air and the fly touched down on the river without splashing I watched it drift toward me with the current and was so confident that a trout would rise to it that my hands trembled. But no trout rose. I caught no trout that trip nor during the half-dozen I took to the Boardman on my own that May and June.

I became so frustrated finally that I abandoned the river one bright morning and drove to a commercial trout pond where, for $1.25 per pound, no license required, I was allowed to stand on the edge of a concrete basin and cast over trout that were considerably less demanding than the brown trout of the Boardman. I waited until the attendant had walked off, then stripped line from my reel, took a deep breath, and began backcasting like crazy.

The casting motion of my rod arm summoned fish like a dinner gong, and they rushed me in a mass. I caught fifteen rainbows in fifteen casts. The house rules made it clear that this was not catch-and-release fishing. I was responsible for keeping and purchasing every fish I caught. Unknown to the attendant, however, I had pinched the barb closed on the black gnat wet fly I was using, and whenever he was not looking I would play a fish until it was tired, then throw slack in my line and the fish would shake free of the hook. One two-pound trout was hooked too deeply to get loose and I ended up buying it. I also caught a sixteen-inch brown trout that attacked my fly like a vicious ferret. The attendant said it shouldn't have been there and must have "escaped" from the creek that supplied the pond with water. He let me keep it, no charge.

We were not troubled youngsters. In an era when many of our classmates were the products of dissolving families, Doug, Russ, and I were the outsiders, brought up in wholesome, healthy environments by relatively happy, well-adjusted parents who thought highly of us and cared about our

welfare. We were good students, or were at least obedient
students who did what was expected of us, and were well
groomed and well dressed. It was embarrassing to be so good,
and in compensation we rebelled in small ways—skipping
class to go fishing (on a day when we knew there would be
no exams), smoking Swisher Sweets at the drive-in theater,
smuggling a single tall-boy of Budweiser to a Friday night
football game and sharing it among three or four of us.

In our crowd only Wesley had grown up in unhappy
circumstances. His parents divorced when he was young,
and he lived now with his father, who owned our town's
lone taxi. It was an unthriving business—the cab was rusted
and had a bad muffler—and we knew Wesley's father spent
his evenings drinking beer at the Sail-Inn, and much of each
day drinking coffee in Stacey's restaurant downtown. There
was little call for cabs in Traverse City then. Wesley's mother
was never mentioned.

I don't know how Wes entered our circle of friends. In
a high school clotted with cliques it was difficult to infiltrate
certain groups, though ours was less discriminating than
most. Wes was lively and witty, but because he was so different from us there were days when we ganged up to humiliate
him in small ways. Yet we were careful. He was small but
had a terrible temper. He never hesitated to fight larger boys
if they provoked him, attacking with such violence that they
often backed off in alarm. If he lost a fight he never asked for
sympathy or doctoring; if he won we swaggered with him,
enjoying the victory in proxy.

One day at school, lounging at a table in the student
commons, Wes suggested we sneak in some night and fish
the ponds in Oleson's buffalo fields. We agreed to the idea
instantly. We agreed instantly because we did not for a moment believe we would ever actually do it. Such acts were for
the outcasts who tattooed themselves with straight pins and
india ink, who smoked cigarettes on the sidewalk outside
school, who in the afternoons came to class drunk or high.
We knew them from a distance, knew they smashed their
cars into trees, had girlfriends who became pregnant and

fathers who beat them, had mothers who worked as wait-resses and dyed their hair approximately blond. They were troublemakers, and Doug, Russ, and I were so unaccustomed to making trouble that we assumed we were incapable of it. No police officer would ever visit our parents, we knew, no judge would ever know us by name.

Yet the summer between our junior and senior years, nudged along by Wes and fueled by boredom and raging hormones, we began making serious plans for an expedition to the Buffalo Ponds. We learned that an old man in a house across the highway worked as the caretaker and night watch-man of the farm and that it was his job to prevent anyone from entering the property. To us it seemed the bison were the real watchdogs of the place. They stared defiantly at tour-ists who lined up to photograph them through the fence beside the highway, and dreamed, you could imagine, of a time without fences. We noticed that each evening the herd congregated beside the wooden feed bins near the highway and seemed to spend the night gathered there as if for com-fort. Forty acres away, isolated safely, was the string of ponds.

One night, when the moon was a high sliver without much light, we parked my father's Buick in the lot of a car dealership that backed up to the far corner of the buffalo fields. We sat in the car for a few minutes to be sure no lights swept our way (we had a fear of police cruisers appearing suddenly in the dealership driveway), then gathered our fishing tackle from the trunk and set off across the meadows. Immediately below the parking lot, lit in the blue, moonlike glow of the pole lamps, was a tiny stream, a tributary of Kid's Creek so narrow we did not need to jump it. We stepped across.

The fence around the buffalo fields rose six feet and was capped with a double strand of barbed wire. We climbed it at a corner, where the wires turned away at right angles from the corner post. At the top we held the barbed wire with our fingertips, dropped our rods on the other side, vaulted over, and were inside.

Across the fields we could see the dark shapes of shrubs and small trees. Each looked like a menacing bull bison. The ground was cropped close by the grazing of the animals, and was dotted with droppings. Evidence of our crime soon filled the treads of our tennis shoes. We jumped across Kid's Creek where it wound shallow and glinting across the pasture, then followed it downstream past the shadowy, tree-lined ovals of the ponds. We went straight to the lowest pond first, guessing it would be the deepest and the most likely to hold big trout.

Wes, equipped with a spinning rod and a large, fluorescent Mepps spinner, made the first cast, his lure fluttering out and landing on the far side of the pond. He was the least reverent and the most pragmatic angler among us and cared nothing for subtleties of method: He wanted fish and lots of them.

Before I could string the line through the guides of my fly rod, Wes hooked a sixteen-inch rainbow and dragged it to shore. We had agreed to release every fish so that if we were caught we could be charged only with trespassing. Wesley unhooked the trout and tossed it into the water as if it were an undersized bluegill.

I tied a white cork popper to my leader, reasoning that if it was visible to me it would be visible to trout. It was my first attempt at fly fishing at night, and I was surprised to

discover that without all the distractions of daylight my casting seemed to improve. The popper gurgled across the water, opening a tiny wake of reflection. Trout did not demolish it at every cast, as I had assumed they would. I cast a half-dozen times before the first rainbow slashed at the fly. When the next two or three trout all measured the same length we became restless and moved up to the second pond.

I had more difficulty there because the row of cedars crowded the shoreline, making it difficult to cast. Wes quickly hooked a good fish that ran and leaped loudly, pulling line from his reel. When Wes led it into the shallows, we discovered that the large spinner was far down in the trout's throat and it was bleeding from the gills. It measured just over twenty inches. Wes announced he was keeping it.

We soon figured out that the ponds held separate size classes of trout. In the first and lowest were sixteen-inchers, in the second twenty-inchers. As quickly as we made that discovery we ran to the third and final pond.

It was the largest of the three. The cedars grew close to the water at the upper end, but at the lower, where the deepest water must have been, the bank was open and grassy. Unprotected by trees we were self-conscious and kept looking back at the brightly lit houses across the road. In one of them we could see a large-bellied man in a white T-shirt walking back and forth in front of a television set.

I cast and retrieved hurriedly, but nothing happened.

"Maybe it's empty," someone suggested.

"Nah," Wes said. "They're in here." He cast, muscling the rod the way he always did, trying to reach farther than he was capable of reaching. At the end of a long cast, while his lure was passing through the deep water near the dam, he hooked something big that put a dangerous, throbbing bow in his rod. Whatever it was, it stayed deep and was too large to be forced to the surface. It traveled up and down the far shore a few times. Wesley's rod groaned with the strain. After a while the line simply gave out, breaking at the lure, and Wes reeled in the slack.

That was enough. As far as Russ, Doug, and I were

concerned the expedition was a success. But Wes was not satisfied. I could hear it in his voice when we tried to get him to hurry and he said, "Wait," hissing it, impatient, a tone that seemed to specify everything that was wrong with our cautious, tentative approach to life. "Come with me," he said. "There's something I want to do."

We followed reluctantly. He walked boldly along the edge of the ponds, in the open, while we skulked in shadows, whispering in urgent voices for him to take cover. He stopped at the small dam at the end of the first pond. Wooden planks had been placed across the outlet to block the flow of water. Wes lowered himself next to the dam, gripped the top plank in his hand, and pried it off. He then pried the next plank. Water spilled through the gap. He pried another plank away and water exited in a condensed deluge. I'm sure that if we had stayed to watch we could have seen the surface of the pond lowering, revealing wet fringes of shoreline that gleamed in the faint light. Wesley laughed. Doug grabbed his arm, but he yanked free and pried at the last plank, wrenching it until it lifted away. Now the water poured out and shot upward in a rooster tail where it struck the streambed below. It sprayed over Wesley. He stood in the spray, arms spread, laughing.

We ran. We did not look back or wait for him. We ran for the fence.

Later, sitting in the car, it seemed funny. We all laughed then. Wes, his jeans soaking water into my father's upholstery, seemed to be laughing at us. We had run ahead of him across the fields, but we knew that it was we who could not keep up with him. He had walked at his own pace, slowed by his wet clothing and by the trout he insisted on carrying back. He had placed the fish with the rods in the trunk of the car. Now it was time to go home. I started the car and was backing around when the deputies arrived.

They caught us in the beam of a spotlight mounted on the door of their car. Even the patrol car seemed wary, pulling slowly into the parking lot. Both deputies stepped out and walked toward us, their hands resting on their belts.

I knew with heart-sinking certainty what would happen. We would be asked for identification, for proof of insurance and registration, for an explanation of what we were doing there. Then, of course, we would be asked to open the trunk. There was no escaping it. The officers would assume we were up to no good and that the evidence was hidden in the trunk.

"What are you boys doing here?"

I was the driver, it was up to me to answer. "Fishing," I said.

"Fishing. Where?"

"In that creek down the bank there."

We could see it from the car, a pathetic trickle lit by the parking lot lights, canopied with field grasses.

"That little creek? What do you catch in a little creek like that at night?

"Steelhead."

"Steelhead."

"Yes. Big lake-run rainbow trout. They run up the Boardman, then come up Kid's Creek to here. You can catch them at night."

"Did you catch any?"

Wesley, Doug, and Russ swiveled their eyes at me in alarm. They were afraid I would lie.

"One," I said. "It's in the trunk."

"Let's take a little look-see."

Lying on a heap of newspapers, surrounded by rods and waders and landing nets, was Wesley's twenty-inch rainbow. The deputies seemed surprised to see it. "Steelhead," I said.

We were saved by their ignorance. If they had been fishermen they would have known that no steelhead of that size would be in a Lake Michigan tributary in July, and that even if one happened to be there it was unlikely it could be caught by legal methods at night, in a creek twenty-four inches wide.

"Well, okay, I guess. But look here. You boys park somewhere else from now on. They've had trouble with kids stealing hubcaps and batteries in this lot. Stay away from here."

"Yes sir."

I started to close the trunk. The second deputy, who had not spoken until then, suddenly stopped my hand and said, "That's a legal fish, isn't it?"

Wes, drawing on all the sarcasm he could fit in his small body, said, "No, it's too small."

The deputy looked at him sharply, then backed down.

"You boys better be moving along," he said. "Next time find a better place to park."

"We will, officer."

"We will, officer," Wesley said, mimicking me.

For weeks afterward we caught rainbow trout from the creek. They were fat, witless fish that measured sixteen or eighteen inches and weighed two pounds each. If you cast a muddler minnow or a grasshopper or a worm into any pool between the highway and the state hospital a trout would chase it, sometimes in its eagerness leaping clear of the water to capture the bait. Each of us caught perhaps a hundred trout, and kept every one. Our parents were flabbergasted. They could not believe our skill. But we knew skill was not involved.

We fished Asylum Creek every day that summer until the trout were gone.

FISHING THE JAM

My father never learned the art of snagging salmon. I realize now that is to his credit, but when I was seventeen and suffering from a serious case of blood lust, it was a matter of some embarrassment. My friends and I had become aficionados of the unadorned treble hook and I had little patience for a man who hardly tried. He stayed home that fall and fished alone for walleyes in Long Lake. I joined the crowd at the Boardman River in Traverse City and learned a hard lesson.

The river had filled suddenly and unexpectedly with so many coho salmon, a new and exotic species in our part of the world, that everywhere we looked we saw enormous fish porpoising, swirling, leaping clear of the water to land in great side-smacking explosions. It was hardly possible to drag a lure through the water without hooking one. My friends and I, drunk with abundance, figured we could be forgiven if we killed a few more than our share, or if we forgot—temporarily, temporarily—such concepts as restraint and honor and sportsmanship.

It was the beginning of our last year of high school and we were eager to be released to the broad freedoms of adulthood. Every afternoon, the moment the final bell rang, we ran for the parking lot and drove Doug's rust-shot Torino straight to the river. There, at least, we were equals to anyone. On the water we had already graduated to a bigger world.

We recognized many of the cars parked beside the bridge. Other students had skipped school, had been here all day, and would have raked the Willow Hole clean by noon. Below the bridge, the hardcore regulars, the Men, stood in ranks along shore. They crowded each other, their thickets of rods in constant up-and-down motion. They used surf-casting outfits with thirty-pound-test line and cast their heavily weighted lures like they were heaving anvils into the river.

We hurried into our waders, grabbed our spinning rods, and raced down a trail almost nobody else used, beneath tag alders and blackberry brambles, over piles of crumbling yellow bricks and tangles of the discarded monofilament line that stretched in coils and snarls from Union Street Dam to the mouth of the river. We busted out onto the riverbank. The pool was deserted. Fishermen were upstream and down—we could hear a wailing drag, the crash of a leaping salmon, shouts and curses and laughter—but somehow, this spot, *the* spot, had been left to us.

Doug, careless with knots and other trivial matters, was rigged first. Before he could cast, a large salmon broke the water at midstream; another swirled close to the bank. Doug tossed his Spider out and across, allowed it to sink the necessary three-count, then began the old jerk-and-haul.

"You bozos better hurry," he said. "Unless you want to watch me catch all the—Whoa!"

He was into one already. It ran downstream, his rod skewed low and rigid, the reel shrieking, the line tearing across the river so fast it raised a trail of mist on the water. Suddenly the fish came up: somersaulting in its own spray, arching and flexing, crashing back into the river. It was hooked in the back. Good spot. It gave the fish leverage but did not disable it with pain.

We had forgotten the net. Russ and I refused to go back to the car. Doug screamed at us to go but we ignored him.

I cast my Spider and let it sink. One-thousand-one, one-thousand-two, one-thousand-three. Wait any less and the hook would be pulled over the tops of the salmon. Wait any longer and it would get wedged in rocks, driven into a log, or tangled permanently in the monster-snarls of line that had been growing like fungus on the bottom since the run began. Yank and reel, sidearm to keep the hook low. Yank and reel. No resistance to speak of, just the number 2 treble and the quarter-ounce bell sinker streaking through the water. Yank and Whoa! It ran instantly, the rod maxing out, the fish up and leaping before I could warn Doug to watch his line. He hadn't landed his ten-pounder yet, and mine, twelve pounds at least, crossed his line and his crossed mine and mine crossed his again. Then the two salmon plowed off in opposite directions and the lines broke almost simultaneously, like rapid-fire gunshots.

Doug blamed me, of course. He had a scrub brush of hair growing straight up from his forehead, like he'd been shocked. When he was angry he would push his glasses up on his nose; they'd slide down and he would push them up again. Russ, meanwhile, cast into the pool and on the first yank was into a fresh-run eight-pounder that blasted out of the water almost the instant the hook bit. Doug, to cool off, left for the car to get the net. I landed Russ's fish for him, waiting until he led it into shallow water and then placing my foot beneath its belly and booting it up on the bank. When Doug returned with the net, Russ had his fish hung on the stringer in the shallows, and I was into another, a coho that might have gone to ten pounds except that it was hooked in the absolute maximum leverage point of the tail and I didn't have a chance. It made a V-wake for Lake

Michigan and kept going even after my line popped fifty yards downstream, where the fast water began at the Front Street Bridge.

The newspapers called it Coho Fever. It appeared shortly after the salmon began congregating near the mouth of the Platte River in northwest lower Michigan in 1967, eighteen months after they had been planted by the Michigan Department of Natural Resources in an effort to revitalize a Great Lakes fishery that was suffering, to say the least. Once considered sport-fishing heaven, the Great Lakes had become a wasteland. Parasitic sea lampreys had wiped out the lake trout, and massive schools of alewives—small, shadlike bait fish that had the unpleasant habit of dying by the millions every summer and fouling the beaches—were nearly all that thrived in the lakes.

Nobody knew if the salmon would feed on the alewives, or even if they would survive in the big lake. But when adult fish appeared in Platte Bay late that summer all expectations were surpassed. They had grown an astonishing eight to fifteen pounds in less than two years, and were returning to their parent stream in numbers that even the most optimistic fisheries biologists had not dreamed of. The fever became an

epidemic. Mile-long lines of vehicles waited to use the ramps giving access to the lake, and frenzied anglers launched their boats the way a dump truck unloads a full bed of refuse: backing up fast to the ramp and hitting the brakes. They then would park in the loose sand along the road, getting their vehicles stuck and abandoning them there. Later, when salmon moved up the rivers, the fever moved up with them. I caught a bad dose of it.

We were not prepared for the salmon. Our equipment was inadequate and we had no idea what techniques might catch the fish. A few people were looking to the Pacific Northwest and Alaska for precedent, and a very few were convinced that the salmon could be caught in the rivers on conventional tackle, but most anglers believed that once a salmon entered a river it would show no interest in lures or bait. It was thought that since the fish would inevitably die after spawning, we were justified in harvesting them with any method that worked. That attitude was endorsed by the Department of Natural Resources, and snagging was legalized on virtually every Michigan river those first few years. It became the standard tactic of most river fishermen.

In the Boardman, in Traverse City, hundreds of salmon were stacked in every pool from the mouth of the river to the Union Street Dam, a distance of about a mile. Snaggers would fill their five-fish limit, carry the salmon home in the trunks of their cars, then return to fill another limit. Catches of twenty fish a day were not unusual at first, before the competition got intense. By then it was as entertaining to watch the action as it was to participate in it. Fishermen unequipped for the strength of the salmon watched their reels explode and their rods shatter. Full-grown men leaped into the river to do battle hand-over-hand with salmon that had smashed their equipment. Fishermen standing elbow-to-elbow at the hot spots became involved in incredible tangles of line when hooked fish ran parallel to shore. Harsh words were exchanged. Fights broke out.

My friends and I learned fast. We used sturdy fiberglass

spinning rods and reels with smooth drags. Many of the snaggers preferred twenty- and even thirty-pound-test line, but we chose to use eight-pound test, willing to lose a few fish in exchange for the greater casting accuracy of the lighter line. Refining our techniques, we became proud young masters of snagging. We devised our own snagging lure—the Silver Spider—a treble hook with a heavy bell sinker attached underneath by a few twists of copper wire. It was a deadly, streamlined weapon that rode through the water hooks upright, ready to impale anything in its way.

Doug, Russ, and I hooked six fish in six casts. We had never seen the pool so full of salmon. But our activity attracted the attention of fishermen above and below us and they were closing in. Russ made a hurried cast and lofted his Spider over a willow branch. Doug, laughing, cast sidearm to put his hook beneath the same branch, hauled back once, and nailed a big, silver female that did a tail-walking routine the length of the pool. Seven for seven.

I made a cast, jerked, reeled up, jerked, and was into another fish. Eight for eight. After hundreds of pounds of snagged salmon I knew immediately not only the size of the fish but approximately where it was hooked: head, side, belly, or tail. This was a small one, maybe three pounds, hooked amidships. I wasted no time, simply derricked it in and dragged it onto the beach.

But it was not a salmon. It was a brown trout, vivid with spawning colors, with the hooked jaw and thick body of a healthy, mature adult—the largest and most beautiful trout I had ever hooked. I had snagged dozens of salmon and never felt the slightest remorse, treating them like throwaways, like objects of commerce given out to promote business. But this was different. This was a wild, natural fish, here for a purpose that had nothing to do with the circus atmosphere of the mock run of salmon. I had seen other trout snagged. A few steelhead had entered the river, and they were sometimes snagged, netted, and hurried to car trunks by men and boys who laughed about their indiscretion. Possessing snagged trout was unlawful, of course, but the law seemed to be held in abeyance those days.

I was determined to release the trout. I kneeled and removed the hook carefully. The wound seemed shallow, harmless.

"What you got there?"

I looked up, expecting a conservation officer. He was a man, perhaps forty years old, dressed in street clothes and wearing aviator's sunglasses. Not a conservation officer. Not a fisherman, either.

"Brown trout. I hooked him accidentally."

"Accidentally. Sure."

"I'm going to let him go."

"Why let him go? I'll take him."

I had noticed people like him lingering on the fringes. They were not fishermen, but they liked to watch. Sometimes they cadged a salmon or two from the fishermen whose freezers were already filled.

"I have to let him go."

"Seems like a shame. A waste."

"He was hooked lightly. He'll be okay."

I noticed his trousers were too long and the cuffs had frayed where they dragged on the ground. He wore black, heavy-heeled leather shoes caked with mud. I looked up and he was smiling at me. He never quit smiling.

"It's just going to die anyway," he said.

"No it's not," I insisted. I was growing uneasy. I wanted to release the trout and see it swim away as if nothing had happened.

The man shrugged, smiling, and stepped forward. He raised his foot and brought it down heel first on the trout's head, crushing it into the gravel. The body jumped once, then was still.

Sliding his hand under the gill-plate, he lifted the fish. "See?" he said. "It's just gonna die anyway."

I did not know it yet, but I was finished as a snagger. I

would go home that evening not sure about what had happened, knowing only that the fun had gone out of it. In a few years the Department of Natural Resources would virtually abolish snagging anyway, limiting it to a few short stretches of the larger rivers, and eventually it would be banned altogether. Anglers, forced to experiment, would discover that salmon in rivers could be caught after all on lures, bait, and flies.

Standing beside the river, watching the man walk off with the mutilated trout, I realized my enjoyment had been tainted all along. We had caught fish, many fish, but it had been an empty exercise. Intent on having fun, we had failed to consider fair play. It was obscenely easy to convert abundance into waste, but at some point—and now it seemed inevitable—there must always be a reckoning.

LAKE TROUT NIGHTS

There were phantoms in the bay that fall. They swam into the shallows at night, attracted to lights on piers and breakwalls, and because they moved without haste and glowed with an eerie paleness against the dark water it was easy to imagine they were the ghosts of lake trout killed in the 1940s and 1950s, when overfishing, lampreys, and alewives had ruined the Great Lakes fishery. But by 1970 the lakes had been restored to something like their former greatness, as full of life as anyone could hope, and what looked like phantoms those nights in November turned out to be flesh and blood.

We first heard rumors about them from anglers who said lake trout were being caught at night in the harbor at Leland, on the Lake Michigan shore of the Leelanau Peninsula. But Leland was a thirty-mile drive from our house and there was so much good fishing closer to home that my father and I felt no urgency to go there. We had plenty to distract us: Steelhead were in the rivers, woodcock and grouse were in the poplar coverts, lake-run brown trout and king salmon could be caught from the piers and stream mouths around Traverse City.

But we kept hearing stories about the strange run of lake trout in Leland and finally could not resist the novelty. On a Friday night in late October my father and I loaded our gear in the car and drove over to investigate.

The place was a madhouse. Hundreds of anglers, their rods bristling over the water, lined both sides of the river the short distance from the dam at Main Street to where it emptied into the harbor. Many of the fishermen had climbed onto the decks of the commercial fishing trawlers and private pleasure boats moored along the edges of the river, ignoring prominent signs forbidding it, and here and there arguments were in progress between boat owners and fishermen. Arguments were in progress as well among fishermen themselves, those whose lines had tangled, or who had lost brief battles with trout because someone cast over their lines or stabbed ineptly with landing nets and panicked the fish, allowing them to get away. The area was bright with streetlights and looked like a gaudy, chaotic, low-budget carnival.

As we walked along the river we were told the lakers were hitting on spawn bags fished on the bottom and on a deadly little jigging lure called, inelegantly, the Swedish Pimple. The lures were supposed to be most effective fished vertically from the bank or from the boats along the river. But though we watched a dozen trout landed, none were hooked in the mouth. Most had been snagged in the belly or side by the sleek jigs.

Nobody seemed to know why the lake trout were there, if they had been coming in like that for years, or if it was a recent phenomenon. Some anglers theorized the lakers had come into the river to feed on the loose roe of spawning salmon and brown trout. Others argued that the lakers had been planted there as fingerlings and were simply returning to their parent stream to spawn. But when female lake trout were caught they were found to carry immature spawn, and biologists insisted that lake trout spawned late in November over rocky shoals in the open lake. The only certainty was that the trout were there, in enormous numbers, and as far as anyone knew (or was telling) they had not been there in previous years.

My father had no interest in joining the fray below the dam, so we took a walk out onto a deserted dock in the harbor. At the end of it, beyond the marina attendant's shack and gas pumps, a single neon light on a high pole lit a circle in the water. We had the entire dock to ourselves and could look across the open water of the harbor and see the crowds of people lining the river.

My father reached the end of the dock first, looked down for a moment, then turned quickly and walked back toward me.

"Don't do anything to attract attention," he said. "Stay out here and look casual. I'm going to the car to get the rods."

I walked to the end of the dock and looked down. At first I saw nothing but the startling clarity of the water; in the light of the neon bulb overhead it was blue. Then I saw

movement, pale objects drifting past, and realized I was seeing a pod of six or eight lake trout, so light in color they appeared to glow. They swam slowly past the end of the dock toward the river, turned in a broad circle, and returned the way they had come, as if following an invisible track. Then I saw six more; then twelve. Suddenly there were dozens—hundreds—circling in the open water off the end of the dock.

My father, strolling casually, returned with our rods. We rigged up, aware that fishermen at the mouth of the river were glancing toward us. "This won't last long," Dad said. We threaded small spawn bags on our hooks and weighted the line a foot or two above the hooks with split shot. Taking our time, hoping to give the impression we had no targets, we cast over the cruising trout.

In the clear water the balls of orange roe glowed as they sank. It was impossible to tell if the lake trout noticed them. The fish seemed to swim past without looking at anything, certainly without the appearance of hunting or feeding. We held our rods lightly, certain we would have strikes. When nothing happened we reeled in and cast again.

My father waited to cast until he saw trout coming, then lobbed his bait so it would descend directly in front of them. He had removed a large split shot and replaced it with a tiny one just heavy enough to make it possible to cast. The tiny orange ball sank slowly. A trout approached, swimming with methodical, lazy undulations. There was a slight, barely perceptible change in its motion, as if it had stumbled, and a brief flash of white. The flash of white was the inside of the trout's mouth, revealed as it opened to engulf the bait. My father struck back with his rod.

The trout fought deep, lunging and rolling. Only when it had been brought near the surface did it make anything like a run, enough to force my father's spinning reel to give up some line. By the time we netted it, a fine eight-pound fish, a half-dozen other fishermen had reached the dock and more were on the way.

"Are they out there?"

"Jesus, yes. Look at 'em."

There was no pretense involved. Swedish Pimples splashed the surface and were retrieved in vicious jerks. Nobody hooked a thing. The trout disappeared. In a few moments, so did we.

Not long after our night in Leland, lake trout were discovered cruising along the breakwall at Clinch Park in Traverse City. The remainder of that fall the rails of the breakwall were lined every night with fishermen standing shoulder-to-shoulder casting sleek jigs into the deep water on the bay side of the wall. You could always see how productive the previous night's fishing had been by going down to the breakwall in the morning. If there was time on our way to school my friends and I pulled into the parking lot behind the zoo and walked out on the broad walkway capping the breakwall. Monofilament hung in snarls from the power lines between the pole lamps along the wall, and discarded lure packages and bait containers were scattered on the cement walkway. Wherever a trout had died the spot was marked with a plate-sized pool of drying blood and slime. Gulls hopped around the blood or hovered just overhead in the wind.

Doug, Russ, and I had fished there a few times, lured by the chance to catch the big trout on light line. But the scene always appalled us. We were not being righteous—we had, after all, just spent a good part of the autumn snagging salmon from the Boardman River—but there was something so blatant and ugly in the behavior of the people crowding the rails of the breakwall that we found ourselves driven away. Most of the lines cast from the breakwall were tipped with snagging lures of one sort or another, most of the anglers activating them used the same gung-ho heave and reel tactic that was so effective in snagging salmon. When we heard the cry "Fish on!"—and crying out was necessary to clear nearby lines quickly enough to avoid getting hopelessly tangled and starting small wars—we watched snagged lake trout netted quickly by businesslike fishermen who tossed the fish onto the concrete, unhooked the evidence, and clubbed the fish to death so they would not flop back over the edge into the water.

We heard rumors that a few lakers were being taken on spawn bags at the mouth of the Boardman River. The crowd was thinner there, but we stood waist-deep in our waders in the painfully cold water one night and cast hundreds of times without a strike. We finally gave up on it—gave up on lake trout entirely. We went back to fishing the river and the forgotten corners of the bay for steelhead, brown trout, and salmon.

One night Doug and Russ went exploring in a marina a mile up the bay from Clinch Park. We had caught a few trout and salmon from similar spots, and liked to check them now and then for stragglers. This marina, one of several on West Bay, was in a small, man-made harbor big enough for a pair of mooring docks and several dozen boats. Most of the boats had been hauled from the water and stored. The place was empty and dark.

At the entrance to the little harbor was a deep, narrow channel dredged between a spit of land and a wharf. The wharf extended along the front of a warehouse used for storing boats in the winter, and was lit at its end, at the narrowest portion of the channel, by a pole lamp that cast a dome of light on the water. Doug and Russ wandered over to the light and looked down.

They called me about midnight, waking my parents and instigating a minor panic in the household. Doug was so excited he could hardly be understood. But I got the message. Lake trout. Hundreds of them.

We were there before dark the following evening. Doug and Russ had each taken their limit of five lakers the night before and were confident. When I saw nothing in the water I began to doubt them.

"They'll come, just be patient," Russ said.

The trout appeared shortly after dark. They streamed in through the channel, glowing white beneath the lamp, and, like the fish in Leland Harbor, they moved so slowly and mindlessly they appeared to be hypnotized. At first I could only watch in amazement, stunned by their numbers. Hundreds of lake trout weighing six, eight, or ten pounds paraded slowly through the channel, some deep, some barely below the surface, all within fifteen or twenty feet of where we stood above them on the wharf.

Doug and Russ had worked out a technique the night before. They attached tiny spawn bags containing only three or four salmon eggs each to small hooks and flipped them without sinkers into the channel. With no weight on the line they could cast the bait scarcely fifteen feet, but it was far enough to reach the cruising trout. In the blue light from the lamp we could see the spawn as it sank. Trout cruised past in weird somnolence. Every third or fourth cast a sudden, yawning flash of white would appear deep in the water—the inside of a trout's mouth as it opened to take the spawn—and one of us would set his hook.

Lakers are not fierce battlers, and these fought even less fiercely than most, as if their minds were somewhere else. Few made long runs or dramatic struggles. Most fought a dogged, distracted battle, swimming to the bottom of the channel or rising to the surface and rolling over and over until they were spiderwebbed in line. We worked them close to the dock and netted them, or more often laid on our bellies and unhooked them with pliers without lifting the trout from the water. We learned quickly not to put our fingers in their mouths: Those catlike teeth were sharp.

After an hour or two no more trout passed through the channel. By then we had caught our limit and had released many others. We walked along the dock toward the interior of the marina and came upon a strange scene. In a corner of the harbor about the size of an Olympic swimming pool, bounded on three sides by docks and, again, lit by an overhead lamp, hundreds of lake trout swam in a tight, clockwise circle. They were crowded from the surface down to a depth of perhaps eight feet, and swam as if transfixed or drugged in a continuous, unhurried procession around the little bay. Each seemed intent on following the path of the fish ahead of it. Zombie trout. It was possible they were practicing some bizarre spawning rite, yet, as with the fish at Leland, the spawn and milt of the fish we dressed out would prove to be immature. The circling lakers were more reluctant to strike than they had been in the channel, although we continued to hook strays. We tried spinners, spoons, and plugs, but except for occasional—and accidental—foul hooks, the lures were ineffective. Sometimes the trout shied away from the flashing lures; usually they simply ignored them.

We came back, night after night, expecting at any time to find other fishermen had discovered the place and its trout. Within a few nights we were so confident of success we no longer bothered keeping any fish. If our mothers announced that the freezer was empty and the family hungry for baked lake trout it would always be a simple matter to go that night to the marina and catch a brace of five-pounders for the table. We became catch-and-release advocates, not from lofty motives, but because netting, untangling, and unhooking the trout took more time than reaching down to the water to pry the hooks free. Each of us, after all, was interested primarily in catching more fish than the others. If there had been some variety in the trout—occasional twenty-pounders, for instance—we might have competed for trophies. But the size varied little. We caught a few twelve-pounders, but the rest, with monotonous consistency, weighed five to ten pounds. The only mark of our skill was in numbers hooked and released.

The weather, which had been pleasant through the end of October, turned ugly in November. A cold front moved in and we fished in snowstorms, the hard, brittle snow blown in from the lake by wind harsh enough to cut through our clothing. It became so cold that landing and unhooking a fish was an ordeal. But we did not have to suffer long. The trout disappeared. One night we noticed fewer in the marina; the next night there were fewer yet. In another day or two we saw none. It was just as well. Those were school nights. We had been going to class on five or six hours of sleep and the pace was wearing us down.

We vowed to keep the marina a secret among us three.

We swore on it. We clasped hands and promised we would pluck out our own eyes if we ever told another person about the lake trout. But, of course, that vow did not extend to our families. We had been fishing for years with our fathers; we owed everything we knew to them. The last few nights at the marina our fathers and brothers joined us, so there were seven or eight of us instead of three.

Maybe three high-school boys fishing on a quiet wharf at night could fail to attract notice, but eight people could not. Somebody saw us. Or maybe our younger brothers, who had their own circles of fishing buddies who hit the local creeks on bicycles, did what any of us would have done and shared the spot with their friends.

The next year the trout returned in the middle of October. We were waiting. But it was different. The first night three or four strangers showed up on the dock. The next night eight. The third night a dozen. The trout appeared but in fewer numbers and they were skittish. Some nights they began filing through the channel and were met with so many clumsily cast lures that they turned and disappeared back into the deep water. Our fathers abandoned the place, but we stayed on out of a sense of territorial imperative. We were outraged when a group of older boys, seniors in high school, showed up one night with surf rods and twenty-pound-test line and began snagging the trout as they showed up in the channel.

"They'll hit spawn," I said. I, the budding diplomat. My friends backed me up with emphatic nods.

The largest of the intruders looked at me with disgust. "Oh will they, Fuckhead?"

"Yes. You don't have to snag them."

"What if I want to snag them?"

"Then you're spoiling the fishing for everybody else."

He reached me in two strides, grabbed me by the collar, and swung me out until I was leaning over the water.

"How would you like to go swimming, Asshole?"

"I wouldn't like that."

"How would you like to drown?"

"I wouldn't like that either."

"Then shut your fucking mouth."

He swung me back over the dock. His friends were laughing; mine were fishing a discreet fifty feet away. Snagged trout were flopping on the dock. Several men who had been trying without success to catch the lakers with large spawn bags and heavy bell sinkers had changed over to snag hooks. My friends and I were crowded out, forced to fish in an empty and unproductive corner of the marina. Eventually we went home.

In the years to come, lake trout in the Great Lakes, after rebounding spectacularly from the disastrous infestation of sea lampreys in the 1950s, were in trouble again, threatened by commercial fishing and resurging lamprey populations. Fisheries biologists were concerned that there seemed to be almost no natural reproduction of the trout taking place, and that the fish were not growing large. The Department of Natural Resources shortened the season, making it legal to fish for Lake Michigan lake trout only from May through August, eliminating the fall and winter fisheries.

The breakwall at Clinch Park is empty now on autumn nights, and there are no bloodstains on the concrete. The wharf and storage buildings at the little marina where Doug, Russ, and I fished have been cleared and replaced with an office building, and there are ranks of condominiums on the spit of land across the channel. The entire area is fenced against trespassing.

But no matter. The best times don't last, they can't. We had stumbled upon a marvelous, abundant mystery, and came away convinced that there is more to the world than ordinary daylight reveals. I've wondered many times if the lake trout still make their strange, unexplained run under the lights, but I've never gone back to see.

The Hand of
the Earth

On summer evenings when we were fourteen and fifteen years old my friends and I would meet on a grassy hill behind Ken Norris's house or in the meadows near Cedar Lake and camp out. They were the simplest of expeditions, our equipment minimal, our expectations modest. We camped in the open most nights, unrolling our sleeping bags directly onto the dry, coarse field grass, folding our sweatshirts into pillows, and lying beneath the stars talking, counting meteors, and sharing grand dreams. We had reached the age when our lives seemed to stretch ahead like unfurling scrolls and we were sure we knew what was written there. There would be fame and fortune, of course, and freedom and passion. We vowed not to let love or ambition lure us into the clutching traps of adulthood.

We were determined never to marry. We would be bachelor adventurers and dedicate our lives to fishing and hunting.

By our senior year of high school our resolve had faltered only a little. We had girlfriends, but we were careful to avoid the complicated relationships that made virtual married couples of some of our classmates. We resisted entanglements.

I had classes that year with a petite brunette named Gail, whom I'd known off and on since first grade, when she distinguished herself by being the fastest runner in our grade yet refused to run squealing from the boys during the games of chase we played at recess. I remember being impressed by her independence. Now, in high school, we became reacquainted. Sometimes after class we would walk together to the cafeteria or the bus stop or would sit at a table in the student commons and talk about the people we dated and the lives we planned to live when we were out of school. She was determined to never marry, she said, because marriage was death for a woman who intended to have a career, as she did. She wanted to be an architect or an artist. I talked about fishing, baseball, girls, and books. She talked about art, wildflowers, and boys. We spent so much time talking that our friends jumped to conclusions. It made us laugh. We were only friends, after all.

In my circle of bachelor pals it was permitted to occasionally take a girl fishing. We considered it a litmus test of compatibility. Girls who were repulsed or bored or insincere failed. Gail passed with high grades because she went along as an equal, not necessarily to fish, but to be near the water and to talk about things that were important to us. I started thinking of her as one of the gang.

One afternoon I took her to the Platte River and showed her the rudiments of fly fishing. I explained that the flies were intended to imitate insects and pointed out the way small trout sometimes flicked out of nowhere to snatch a drifting fly. She sat on the bank wearing an old baseball cap to keep the sun out of her eyes, and asked questions—thoughtful questions, the kind you don't ask if you're being polite or patronizing. I reached into the water near shore and picked up a rock and showed her the insect larvae clinging to it, explaining that it was a good clue to what the fish might be feeding on. She lifted a rock of her own from the river and held it close to inspect the minute, frantically wriggling nymphs. Then, her curiosity satisfied, she turned away, ignoring me altogether, and began drawing wildflowers in a sketchbook. As she worked, she hummed.

I fished downstream a short distance, came back upstream, fished downstream again, never leaving the same small stretch of river. I felt like a moon unable to escape the gravity of a planet.

Gail sat beside a long, slow, weed-fringed pool where I had caught a few small trout in the past, and where the shore brush was low enough to allow a relatively easy cast. As I fished, mayflies started coming off the water and some decent fish began feeding. With Gail watching I got lucky and made a competent cast with a ragged-looking mayfly imitation. The fly drifted upright on the water for a few feet and a rainbow trout about fifteen inches long rose to it and sucked it in. The trout leaped clear of the water, zigzagged madly among the weeds, leaped again and got off. But I had hooked it. It had been fooled by my presentation and by a fly I had tied myself.

"Did you see that?"

"It was big!" Gail cried, clapping.

She shared my joy. She was generous of spirit. It occurred to me that if I ever got married it would probably be to a girl who wore a baseball cap and wasn't afraid to plunge her hands up to her elbows into cold water.

Gail was no angler, not yet anyway, but she was clear-eyed and clear-headed and had an appetite for seeing new places and learning new things. A Swede who could be infuriatingly practical, she had an uncommon appreciation for all things beautiful and true, and an intolerance for falsehoods, ugliness, and deceptions. Unlike many petite girls, she had never learned to act frail and helpless. Barely five-feet, one-inch tall, she did not know until she was twenty-one years old that she was smaller than the majority of adults. It had never occurred to her. And she was freckled, *dappled*. I teased

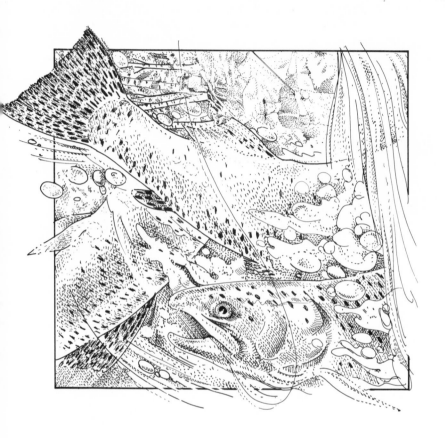

her about having markings like a brown trout, about being the kind of pied beauty Gerard Manley Hopkins had in mind when he wrote, "Glory be to God for dappled things . . . for rose-moles all in stipple upon trout that swim."

"So when are you going to teach me to cast a fly rod?" she asked.

I taught her, as best I could, and she was gloriously indifferent. She did not have an athlete's interest in the mechanics of casting or a predator's interest in the fish. She loved the rivers but the flora along the banks were more interesting to her than the fauna in the water. She had an attitude about fishing that I liked: that it was amusing, slightly ridiculous, saved from total absurdity only if you were passionate about it and not just killing time.

We fell in love watching each other do the things we loved. In her garden, Gail dug in the soil with her bare hands, her jeans soaking through at the knees with ovals of black; when she wiped the hair from her eyes she left a smudge of dirt on her forehead. She made bowls and vases on a pottery wheel, shaping the clay with the same joy the mother of the earth might have felt shaping the world, and did not notice the bits of clay that flew into her hair and spattered her sweatshirt. Her creativity was as messy and undisciplined as nature's. She grew vases and bowls from clay, and nasturtiums and phlox from garden loam, and she did it with the same passion and the same intensity of concentration an angler gives to fishing.

We were married young, barely twenty-one, in a grove of birches beside a Michigan lake, on a day in May so lovely people said it had to be an omen. For the first year we pretended a conventional existence, working throwaway jobs and living in my parents' house on Long Lake, which they had left empty while my father started a business in Kentucky. We saved our money and guarded a secret plan to explore the continent, to travel it with open eyes and no schedule, touching the land, not just seeing it.

The summer of our second year together, we converted a ten-year-old Ford van into a camper, quit our jobs, sold our cars, and headed west. For months we explored the western United States and Canada in what soon evolved into a quest for trout water. Making our way from river to river, we crossed Ontario, Manitoba, Saskatchewan, and Alberta, then turned south into the United States where we kept bumping against the beautiful rivers of Montana, Idaho, and Wyoming. We felt like prospectors discovering gold fields. In early September we found a mother lode in Yellowstone Park, and established a camp in Madison Campground. We were road-weary, we reasoned, tired from the transient life; it would do us good to stay in one spot for awhile. We found a part-time job selling firewood from a private concession in the campground and made enough money to pay for groceries. We stayed for six weeks, until a snowstorm in mid-October drove everyone from the park.

I fished every day of those six weeks. If there is a special heaven for trout fishermen it must be very much like Yellowstone in autumn. Mornings I fished the Madison River near camp, drifting weighted nymphs or huge streamers through pools filled with new browns up from Hebgen Lake. After lunch I took the van and spent the remainder of the day exploring the Firehole, Gibbon, Yellowstone, Gallatin, and other rivers in the park. Gail passed her days hiking, sketching wildflowers, reading, knitting, visiting with neighbors in the campground. Usually it was she who put in our mandatory two hours at the woodshed every afternoon, though I kept promising to take over and do my share.

In the evenings I came home to camp bursting with stories of trout I had caught or lost or seen. There were days on the Madison and Yellowstone when I landed a dozen or more fish over fifteen inches long, and hooked and lost others large enough to compare to the steelhead and salmon of the rivers at home in Michigan. One morning on the Madison I hooked a trout so big its tail looked wide as a shovel blade; it broke off when it stripped line from my reel so quickly that it caused a backlash. I skimmed a muddler minnow across the surface of the Firehole, and a seventeen-inch rainbow chased it exactly like a cat chasing a flannel mouse: pouncing after it and missing, three times in quick succession. The next cast the trout grabbed the fly the moment it touched the water, then leaped completely out of the river four or five times before I landed it.

Gail heard the stories night after night and gradually her expression changed from amusement to curiosity to undeniable interest. "I want to try it," she said finally, and I rigged my extra rod. We set out the next day, together, for the Firehole.

The angling writer Ernest Schwiebert had excellent reasons for calling the Firehole the strangest river on earth. It is bizarre and beautiful, an untamed and inscrutable river flowing among geysers, mud pots, and hot springs, through dangerous steaming meadows, and fed by boiling streams with beds the colors of carnival ice cream. It is a river you might expect to find on Venus and to be inhabited by creatures like those that live in black pools in caves or near thermal vents in the lightless depths of the ocean.

Otherworldly as it seems, the Firehole is grounded firmly on the earth. It's fished hard, but the brown and rainbow trout that live in it are so abundant and grow so quickly in the fertile water you can always find good fish that seem not to have been made skeptical by encounters with artificial flies. Or maybe we were just lucky. We saw few other fishermen in the park that year and had the Firehole mostly to ourselves.

We went to a stretch of river flowing through a meadow, where Gail could cast without worrying about snaring trees and shrubs, and stopped beside a slow, deep pool. In the distance steam rose like enormous feathers. The air smelled of sulphur.

Gail looked through my fly boxes and selected a chewed-up black nymph the size of a cigar butt. We took a few minutes to review the basics of casting, and I left her and walked away downstream.

I had gone only fifty feet when she screamed. I turned and saw the water in the pool erupting, her rod bent down into the river.

"Whoa Nellie! Whoa Nellie!" she shouted, like a greenhorn on a runaway stallion. Her rod pointed straight into the heart of the pool. "Whoa Nellie!" she cried again.

When I reached her she was shaking so hard she could hardly hold her rod. The leader had broken.

"It was a trout," she said. "An enormous, enormous trout. It came up out of the deep water and took the fly. It was huge. I could see its spots. My God, it was enormous."

There had been times in the past when Gail questioned my reasons for fishing. She understood the urge to be near water, to go out early in the morning and see the mist rising above it, to stand and feel the current against your legs and hear the murmuring and chuckling sounds around you. But she never comprehended why I could get so excited about hooking a fish on a tiny lure and pulling it in. Now she knew.

"It felt," she said, "like the hand of the earth reached up and grabbed my line."

MY CLASSIC CANOE

At sixteen years old, when I didn't know the difference between a J-stroke and a spray skirt, and was happy in my ignorance, my friend Tom Zenner and I stayed up all night on a summer camping trip drinking Coke, belching like lumberjacks, and telling lies about our experiences with girls. Late in the night we discovered the shared ambition of canoeing across the wilderness of northern Ontario. We had the same image in mind: paddling in the mist across remote lakes ringed with spruce and tamarack, moose raising their dripping heads from the water as we passed. We saw ourselves clearly, the sleeves of our flannel shirts rolled up, our hair tossed by the wind in a carefully nonchalant way, our eyes bright with strong, keen, faraway looks. We agreed that if we wanted to cut such striking fig-

ures, it was necessary—absolutely essential—that we be paddling a classic canoe.

Classic canoes come in many forms, from cedar-strip to
birch-bark, but in our judgment there was only the classic
wood-and-canvas Old Town. So covetous were we of such
craft that we immediately ordained any wooden canoe an Old
Town, no matter what its make and origin. We knew almost
nothing about them, but a friend, aware of our enthusiasm,
informed us that those old canoes lacked durability and
should always be beefed up with a coat of sturdy, dependable, all-but-indestructible fiberglass.

Fortune tends to grin on worthwhile enterprises: Tom
found our Old Town that very summer. It was resting on the
beach in front of a cottage on Long Lake, across the lake from
where I lived. The canoe's owners agreed we could have it if
we promised to take it quickly and leave no scraps to litter
the beach.

Like any good classic canoe, it had been left untended
for many years. Although stored with the hull turned up to
repel weather, the weather had managed to find its way
inside, and the flanks had long ago burrowed deep into the
damp sand. We excavated as fastidiously as archaeologists,
digging the canoe free on all sides, prying it gently from the
sand, laying it finally across the top of my father's rowboat.
Tom held it in place while I motored at trolling speed across
the lake. We hauled it up from the shore, balanced it on
sawhorses in the middle of my parents' driveway, and went
to work.

The original cane seats were ruptured artifacts; we replaced them with carefully woven white clothesline. We
carved a new thwart from a length of maple and fitted it
between the gunwales. We yanked hunks of dry-rotted cedar
from the hull and replaced them with sections cut from
wooden apple crates borrowed from my father's garage, nail-
ing them in place where we could, otherwise attaching them
with glue and duct tape. It seemed to take no time at all before
we were ready for the final touch.

In those days our favorite source of hunting, fishing,

camping, and boating supplies was Herter's, a famous mail-order house remarkable for the eloquent tag lines in its catalogs: "The Best Bass Lure in the world, GUARANTEED or your Money back with NO QUESTIONS ASKED. Look around and we GUARANTEE you will never find a finer Bass Fishing Lure in the entire world or one that catches such TROPHY LARGEMOUTHS AND LIMITS." We ordered the Finest Fiberglass Boat-Building Kit. It cost forty dollars and was delivered in six weeks. By then it was October, my parents had long ago persuaded me to relocate the canoe and sawhorses behind the garage, and Tom was in school and had a job and a girlfriend and was no longer interested in summer-long canoe trips through the Canadian wilds. "You can keep the canoe," he said. "Just give me back my twenty dollars for the fiberglass kit."

It was raining the day I fiberglassed my canoe, a cold November rain mixed with snow and accompanied by a harsh north wind. Already I had cut and fitted the cloth to the canoe's hull, and now, in the wind, I found masking tape would not hold it in place. Working my way around the perimeter, I splashed resin along the edges to keep the wind from peeling the cloth away.

The first batch of resin, perhaps three-quarters of my

supply, froze to lucid concrete in the bottom of my mother's laundry pail. I had not realized it would harden so quickly. Less than a quarter of the boat was finished, resplendent in gleaming Kelly green. I finished another quarter, but not before the resin thickened to the consistency of Jello and had to be pressed and gobbed into place. It tended to bunch the cloth so that as it dried it looked like the artificial landscapes used by model railroad hobbyists.

I ordered the second fiberglass kit that winter and finished the canoe in the garage. The color of the second batch of resin came out darker than the first, giving the canoe a distinctive two-tone look. I launched it in Long Lake on the first warm spring day and was immediately convinced that a quicker, more lithe boat never plied the waters of our lake. The pure elegance of it enchanted me. Light and lively as a colt, and much faster than any canoe I'd paddled until then, it was my first experience with the efficient hull design of a good canoe.

During the next few years my canoe accompanied me on camping, fishing, and hunting trips everywhere I went in northern Michigan. Our happiest days together were spent in Marquette County, in Michigan's large and largely untrammeled Upper Peninsula, after Gail and I moved there to attend college. In that land of abundant, remote lakes and rivers the canoe gave me mobility, set me free to explore shorelines and river channels, to embark on weekend trips to places few people could reach. Equipped with sleeping bag, pup tent, fishing equipment, topographical maps, and canoe, there was no place in the Upper Peninsula out of my reach. It was intoxicating. I felt invulnerable, capable of surviving—even thriving—in all sorts of upheavals and disasters. I passed the winters planning trips so ambitious I could never complete them in one lifetime.

During the brief, precious summers I often loaded the canoe on my car to go fishing on nearby waters. My friend Dick Armstrong and I took it once to a large impoundment famous for big northern pike. It was located far off the main road, and access was possible at only one spot, a gravel trail at the end of one of the lake's many long, arching bays. The fishing was poor, but we spent our time happily exploring the confusing maze of islands, fishing casually here and there as we traveled. Late in the day we caught a ten-pound northern pike, a large and malevolent fish with a mouthful of razored teeth, that frightened years off our lives when it detonated beneath the floating Rapala I had been splashing out of boredom on the surface beside the canoe. We caught the pike shortly before dark and, in the optimistic manner of anglers everywhere, decided we could catch others. We paddled to the next cluster of lily pads and stumps, cast excitedly, then paddled farther and cast some more—fishing and paddling until it became too dark to recognize landmarks and it occurred to us that we had no idea where we were.

In the dark, a pure and starless darkness so black it was palpable, the lake's shorelines were invisible unless we paddled very close to them, and then they all looked the same. We spent half the night tracing the contours of the shoreline, following all those bays, points, and channels, hoping to stumble upon the access site where we had left the car. We might not have found it until morning except that somebody in a four-wheel-drive pickup attempted to turn around at the end of the road and became stuck in mud. From far across the lake we spotted the headlights reflecting off trees.

When after a few years it came time to leave Marquette, Gail and I realized there was no room for the canoe on the two vehicles loaded with our possessions. Dick and his wife, Trisha, offered to store it in their backyard, and I promised to return in a month or two to retrieve it.

Time passed, and the months became years. I acquired new canoes: expensive, boldly painted creations of Kevlar and Royalex, specialized for solo flat-water touring, for wilderness tripping, for whitewater. I had told Dick to feel free to use the old canoe until I could get up north again, but most of the time it remained stored on horses in his yard, collecting spiders in summer and those enormous Marquette snowdrifts in winter.

After a while Dick stopped asking in his letters when I was coming for the canoe and I stopped making half-hearted plans to return for it. Eventually he wrote to say a neighbor had offered to buy it. The neighbor was a person, Dick said, who appreciated classic canoes. He had been excited to discover it there, neglected in the yard, and had told Dick he wanted to strip it of fiberglass, repair the dry rot, and resurface the hull with fresh canvas. His dream was to take it on long expeditions in Ontario. Dick hoped I didn't mind but he gave it to the guy for nothing.

I'm sure he knows what a bargain he got.

A BIG
TWO-HEARTED
PILGRIMAGE

Spend enough time outdoors in Michigan and sooner or later you cross paths with legends. Many of the most impressive of those paths tend to follow trout streams, and to have been made by one legend in particular: a young, fairly arrogant fellow from Oak Park, Illinois, named Ernest Hemingway. Young Hemingway mapped out much of the best trout fishing in northern Michigan many years ago, and documented it so memorably that on certain waters it is just about impossible to find a stretch free of literary associations. Consequently, some of us, instead of ignoring legends altogether and just going fishing, end up turning our fishing trips into pilgrimages.

Like many people, I first read Hemingway's short story "Big Two-Hearted River" in a high-school English class. It was no accident, of course: Harried instructors learned long ago that they could not keep order in a class forced to plod through *Anna Karenina* or *Jude the Obscure*. What was needed was something short, simple, and compelling, and Hemingway's accessible stories with their compressed, declarative sentences served admirably.

"Big Two-Hearted River" overwhelmed me because I was a passionate trout fisherman and because I happened to be familiar with many of the waters Hemingway wrote about in his early stories—waters he had fished during his summer vacations on Walloon Lake and on trips he and friends took around the northern Lower Peninsula and eastern Upper Peninsula. Besides, "Big Two-Hearted River" brought to life a cherished fantasy of discovering lovely rivers filled with large, surface-feeding trout. It bothered me that Hemingway did not specify the size and species of trout Nick Adams caught, but I became determined anyway to fish the Two Hearted with live grasshoppers on a fly rod, eat peaches from a can, and snuff mosquitoes on the side of my tent with a flaring match. It would be years before I learned how difficult (and dangerous) that can be—the mosquitoes, understandably, will not stand still for an approaching match—and before I learned that Hemingway had duped us with his Two-Hearted River title. The story was about the Fox, not the Two Hearted, and Hemingway, of course, was a liar.

By now the Fox/Two Hearted question creates little debate, but there was a time when it was a matter of some controversy. Graduate students made it the subject of dissertations, and some literary sleuths were said to have traveled to Seney, retraced as closely as possible the course Nick Adams followed over the rolling country north of town, and concluded that it was impossible for him to have hiked in one day to the actual Two Hearted, which is located some twenty miles north of the Fox and flows in the opposite direction, north to Lake Superior.

Author John Voelker, for decades the Upper Peninsula's trout laureate, addressed the problem with characteristic good humor in an essay titled "Hemingway's Big Two-

Hearted Secret." He pointed out that Hemingway merely did what any sensible angler would do—disguise the name of a favorite trout stream to keep the hordes away. The debate may have ended for good when Carlos Baker, in his 1969 biography, reported that Hemingway had once explained the name change was made, "not from ignorance or carelessness but because Big Two-Hearted River is poetry."

It was not poetry so much as the urge to catch big trout that sent me, finally, a few months after moving to Marquette, on my pilgrimage to the Fox. In Marquette, home of Northern Michigan University and the unofficial capital of the Upper Peninsula, I was passing my weekdays in college classrooms and my weekends and holidays exploring nearby rivers and creeks and imagining I was discovering virgin territory. Sometimes it seemed I was. I would stumble on afternoon hatches of mayflies and see brown trout fifteen to twenty inches long rising with naive enthusiasm all around me, on a river less than five miles from the campus in Marquette, and I would have the water completely to myself. If I ever saw another fisherman I considered it a terrible intrusion and the outing was spoiled. It was incredible to me that in the late 1970s, a time when fly fishing was enjoying a popularity boom everywhere in the country, I could find such fine trout waters uncrowded.

In the library I learned of Hemingway's trip to the Fox River in 1919, the year he returned home wounded from Italy. He and his friends Al Walker and John Pentecost camped for a week along the Fox, near the town of Seney, which was once a rough-and-tumble lumber center famed for its brothels and bars, but had been destroyed by forest fires in 1891 and 1895 and was a ghost town by 1919. Hemingway and his friends caught nearly two hundred brook trout that week, including several that reached fourteen and fifteen inches in length. Describing the trip in a letter, Hemingway wrote that one fish that broke his line was the "biggest trout I've ever seen . . . and felt like a ton of the Bricks."

Early on a humid Saturday in June, when I should have been buried beneath the hood of our poor Chevy Bel Air, trying to discover why, after stalling at intersections for the past six months (particularly when it was being driven by Gail, who had not yet mastered the art of braking with her left foot and fluttering the accelerator with her right), it had suddenly come to a more or less permanent stall, I set out instead to hitchhike the seventy-five miles east to Seney and the Fox River. I shouldered a backpack loaded with my sleeping bag, tent, food, and chest waders, and carried my fly rod and a paperback edition of Hemingway's Nick Adams stories. The book was a wise choice; I would do far more reading than fishing that weekend.

The Fox even today has a reputation for brook trout of a size rarely encountered elsewhere in the United States. Fish fifteen to twenty inches long are taken with fair regularity, primarily by locals with a knack for drifting nightcrawlers through the deep pools downstream from Highway M-28. Some of those blunt-bodied trout, their spots highlighted with hobby paint, have been mounted and hung on the walls of area service stations and tackle shops. Ask attendants where the fish were caught and they're likely to avoid your eyes and mumble the names of remote Canadian rivers. Don't believe a word of it. Such trout can still be found in the Fox, though not in the numbers of even a few years ago. The predations of those local trophy hunters have had an impact.

It took me most of the morning to reach Seney, in three rides, including an unforgettable thirty-five-mile hitch from Munising to Seney through the infamous Seney Stretch— twenty-three miles of straight-as-an-arrow highway through a monotonously uniform region of wetlands and tamarack stands—in a pickup truck driven by a skinny, wild-eyed old man who looked like one of the weather-beaten cowboys on the covers of my grandfather's *Western Horseman* magazines. He confessed he was just coming off a three-day drinking binge and apologized for the odor of vomit rising from the floorboards, then proceeded to tell story after story about his youth as a lumberjack in the Upper Peninsula. He had once walked all twenty-three miles of the Seney Stretch at night, after missing his ride back to the lumber camp at the end of

a weekend of drinking in Seney. He tried to hitchhike, he recalled, but in those days traffic was rare as pocket money (his words) and he was forced to walk the entire distance, arriving in camp barely in time to eat breakfast and follow the crew to the woods. He invited me, when we reached Seney at 11:00 in the morning, to join him for a drink at the tavern. In a burst of rare good sense I thanked him, but declined.

Seney today is a crossroads village containing a couple of gas stations and several restaurants, motels, and taverns strung out along M-28. The bridge over the Fox River is a quarter-mile west of most of that industry, as if the town, when it was rebuilt after being leveled by forest fires in the 1890s, was shifted slightly askew by a surveyor's miscalculation. There are no signs of fire now, but if you travel north parallel to the river along County Road 450, you eventually reach an area of uplands known as the Kingston Plains, where treeless, rolling hills are dotted with the dry and silver stumps of ancient pines, many still charred at the edges from forest fires.

I had expected the river to be clear and lively, bubbling over bright cobblestone. Upstream would be a stretch of meadow water where large trout rose to grasshoppers and, beyond it, the river would disappear into a dark swamp that promised even larger trout.

Instead the Fox was small, choked with fallen trees, and flowed sluggishly through dense growths of tag alders. The water was discolored, a blend of silt and swamp drainings, and passed with little vitality over a bottom of soft sand. Several days of rain had raised and muddied the water, and the waist-high grasses below the bridge were still soaked as I waded through them to get a better look at the river.

Growing up in northern Michigan, I got to know biting insects intimately. I prided myself on my ability to tolerate gnats and black flies, and was a recent convert to a mystical theory with native American roots about the powers of indifference and serenity to repel mosquitoes. But I had never seen mosquitoes like those that rose that day from the weeds and grasses along the Fox River. They were larger and more aggressive than the bugs of ordinary experience. Desperate to get at my blood, they surrounded me in a dense, whining, frenzied cloud. My spray repellent was useless. Any insects that might have been repelled were forced toward me by those behind. Even when I sprayed the aerosol directly at them they scarcely altered their flight. They absorbed the poison and developed genetic immunity right before my eyes.

My serenity punctured, I panicked and ran north, upstream, in the direction Nick Adams had hiked. By now every mosquito in the area was alerted and there was no outrunning them. I met a man on the road wearing netting over his head and carrying an impressively stout bait-casting rod. I asked in passing how the fishing was. Terrible, he said.

That decided it. I turned around, ran back to the highway, and hitched a ride west with a young family in a Toyota. They were from Wisconsin and until the mosquitoes ran them off had been camping at the state park near Tahquamenon Falls. I squeezed into the back seat with the two young sons, whose faces were inflamed with insect welts. The parents wanted local color. I told them the old man's tale about the Seney Stretch, and explained that the river they had just crossed, the Fox, was the model for the famous Hemingway story "Big Two-Hearted River." The information seemed to disappoint them.

They let me out along the Lake Superior shoreline near Munising. I hiked a half-mile down the shore, set my tent on the beach in the perpetual, bug-free wind, and passed the remainder of the weekend reading Hemingway's stories and watching waves collapse. I never uncased my fly rod.

BROOK TROUT IN
TRAVER COUNTRY

The Upper Peninsula of Michigan—or the U.P. as it is known by everyone who lives there—is one of those rare places where it is still possible to find lakes and ponds that have never been named. Many of those anonymous waters are seldom visited by humans, being tucked away in valleys too steep or boggy to be accessible even in four-wheel-drive vehicles or too far from roads to be easily reached on foot. Most, at one time at least, were inhabited by brook trout, though a mania for diversification swept the peninsula a few decades ago and many former brook trout waters are now home to walleye, pike, bass, or muskie. And while the fishing for those hardier and more aggressive species can be extraordinary at times, many anglers will tell you that it is brook trout that reign in the U.P.

It's hardly possible to mention Upper Peninsula brook trout without mentioning John Voelker, the former state Supreme Court justice whose lifelong passion was to fish for the native trout of his homeland and write stories about the experience. He gained world fame as the pseudonymous Robert Traver after the 1958 publication of his novel *Anatomy of a Murder*, a smash success that dominated best-seller lists for months and was made into an Academy Award–winning film starring Jimmy Stewart, Ben Gazzara, and Lee Remick. Voelker's novels, and especially the essays and stories collected in *Danny and the Boys, Trout Madness, Trout Magic*, and *Anatomy of a Fisherman*, celebrate the Upper Peninsula, its people, and its fishing like no other books before or since. Many anglers would argue that Voelker earned a lasting place in the pantheon of fishing writers by composing a brief essay called "Testament of a Fisherman," which says in part, "I fish because I love to; because I love the environs where trout are found . . . because I suspect that men are going along this way for the last time, and I for one don't want to waste the trip . . . and, finally, not because I regard fishing as being so terribly important but because I suspect that so many of the other concerns of men are equally unimportant—and not nearly so much fun." They're the words of one of the most eloquent and joyous voices in the literature of sport.

In his eighty-seven years, from 1904 to 1991, Voelker saw many changes come to the Upper Peninsula, and he was not happy about it. Until the end of his life he drove nearly every day in spring, summer, and fall to his tiny cabin, located on a beaver flooding he always referred to in print as Frenchman's Pond, some twenty miles from his home outside Ishpeming. The long and rambling route he followed to get there was not as enjoyable in his later years as it once had been, reminding him every mile that new construction, widened highways, and razed forests were steadily eating away at the U.P. Much of the remote and isolated country of fifty or more years ago, described so delightfully in the early collection of stories *Danny and the Boys*, has disappeared, gone the way of horse-drawn wagons, moonshine, and iceboxes.

Yet by most standards, the Upper Peninsula remains an uncivilized place. Just a few miles outside the fringe of subdivisions and strip malls bordering the cities of Marquette and Escanaba—with populations of 23,000 and 14,000, the largest communities on the peninsula—the country is wild enough to be home to bear, moose, coyote, and a remnant timber wolf population. Much of the truly wild and remote land is contained within several national forests where the standard road is a muffler-ripping two-track logging trail winding among backcountry lakes, rivers, massive cedar swamps, and forests of hemlock, pine, aspen, and hardwoods. With so much territory to explore it is not surprising that fishing and hunting have remained integral to life in the peninsula. Wherever you go, conversations eventually turn to it.

Everyone seems to have a trophy brook trout story, although those stories tend to become generic and imprecise as soon as you start asking for particulars. A resident once told me about fishing the upper reaches of a river in the western U.P., a place where he said he had caught many fine brookies and had hooked and lost one he swore was two feet long. He said to fish the river effectively it was necessary to get there before daylight in the morning and fish shadowy deep spring holes scattered among the otherwise shallow water in the upper reaches. The big trout would come boiling up from those pools, when they were in the mood, and devour anything you offered them. That was entertaining information, but the moment I tried to learn which stretch of which river he was describing, the conversation shifted to the weather, another subject of perpetual concern to Yoopers, as natives of the peninsula call themselves.

If you're lucky, and don't put on airs, you can sometimes meet local anglers willing to share their knowledge. Residents of the U.P. seem by nature generous and ingenuous people, sincerely concerned that you receive a good impression of their home. During a three-day canoeing and fishing trip a few years ago on the Net River, a small and quick-spirited tributary of the Paint River northwest of the town of Crystal

Falls, several friends and I stopped to rest at a grassy meadow, near a family having a riverbank picnic. Three generations of grandparents, uncles, cousins, in-laws, and children walked over to meet us and asked where we were from, where we were going, and whether we had eaten recently. Against our weak protests we were fed cold beer and platters of batter-fried Lake Superior smelt. Asked how the fishing had been, we admitted we had caught some smallmouth bass, but that we were more interested in brook trout. Maps were pulled out and we were given directions to a half-dozen nearby creeks and ponds where we could expect to find good trout fishing.

In the two years I lived in the U.P., and in the many trips I've made there since, I learned it takes more than a single puny lifetime to untangle the secrets of the place. Like searching for knowledge, the more you learn about the Upper Peninsula the more you realize how little you know. Through hard work and persistence I've become fairly well acquainted with a handful of ponds and a few lengths of river, but it is not nearly enough water to ease the aching awareness of my ignorance. There is so much water, Lord, and so little time.

Inevitably, I've been forced to sink to shrewdness and espionage. The Michigan Department of Natural Resources has since 1972 offered a program designed to reward trophy fish with plaques and certificates. Called the Master Angler Award Program, it is meant to encourage fishermen to come forward with news of the outstanding game fish they catch. The fish must be weighed on certified scales in the presence of witnesses, but otherwise the program is a painless way for successful fishermen to receive recognition for their achievements. At the end of each year a detailed report is compiled, listing who caught what fish, when, with what method of angling, and where. According to those reports, Upper Peninsula waters in recent years gave up such memorable brook trout as a five-pound, fourteen-ouncer from a lake in Ontonagon County; a five-pound, one-ouncer from a lake in Schoolcraft County; a four-pound, six-ouncer from a creek in Delta County; and a four-pound, five-ouncer from a lake in Marquette County. During three days in September, two men reported catching six brookies weighing from two-and-a-quarter to nearly four pounds from a pair of ponds in Schoolcraft and Delta counties.

The most surprising thing about such trout is that they were reported at all. A friend of mine, conservation officer Jim Ekdahl of L'Anse, considers the brook trout category the least reliable in the Master Angler program, primarily because so few U.P. trout fishermen are willing to draw attention to their good trout holes. To demonstrate how tight-lipped some of his neighbors and friends are, Ekdahl likes to tell the story of two fellow conservation officers, brook trout maniacs both, who for years worked as partners in the western U.P. They worked together every day, but spent their free time alone, solitary as old bucks, exploring local rivers and earning wide reputations for catching big trout with small, lip-hooked minnows for bait. And while they were willing to admit their success in catching eighteen- to twenty-inch brookies, and would even share tips on tackle and presentation, they would never, under any circumstances, tell anyone—even each other—where they caught them.

River fishing is a time-honored and productive approach to U.P. brook trout, but there are some anglers who specialize in the peninsula's remote, tiny, backcountry ponds. Some of those ponds are natural lakes, gouged by glaciers ten thousand years ago, cleansed and cooled by springs. Others, perhaps the majority, are the work of beavers, often many generations of beavers. Some of the old beaver dams have rooted into permanency and sprouted maple trees ten inches in diameter. If you manage to find an accessible pond with a good population of brook trout, it is a thing to cherish and defend. Many of the ponds easiest to reach have been fished heavily, and can be recognized by the four-foot-wide trails leading from parking areas beside the highway. Occasionally those ponds will give up an epic twenty-inch brookie, but the serious trout anglers usually avoid them. They prospect, instead, for more private waters.

A neighbor in Marquette once told me that he and a

friend found such a pond and that it was stuffed full with brook trout. The first day they fished it, casting dry flies from the boggy shoreline, they caught and released dozens of trout measuring twelve to sixteen inches long. Unfortunately, the action tailed off after that. It seemed the pond was productive only about one day in seven, and only when insects were present in numbers high enough to tempt the trout to the surface. He recalled watching as a sudden gust of wind bent the tamaracks and spruces along shore, blowing insects from the trees onto the surface of the water. Almost immediately hundreds of trout, looking like a maddened school of blue-fish, churned and slashed the surface. When the insects had been cleaned from the water the trout ceased feeding and two hours of casting failed to bring even a single strike. I suggested the story sounded Traveresque, and my friend nodded sagely and said, "Exactly. The man knows what he's talking about."

The U.P. is Traver country, no doubt about it. You hear echoes of his stories in the voices of the locals, in the names of towns and rivers, in the rivers and ponds themselves. Yet digging through the stories in an effort to unearth Upper Peninsula trouting destinations is a remarkably fruitless activity. Traver could never have been accused of being a kiss-and-tell fisherman. Among a collection of imagined or purposefully misnamed creeks and pools, headed by his beloved Frenchman's Pond, there are few locations you'll find on any map.

If there is one body of water made famous by Voelker, it is the Escanaba River. Stories like "The Intruder," "The Old and the Proud," and "Big Secret Trout" speak of a river rich in mystery and possibility, where brook trout share the water with brown trout of mythic proportions. You might think Voelker has betrayed his own best dictate—never to advertise a good fishing hole—thus inciting whole mobs of pilgrims and trout bums to converge on the river. That is, until you see the Escanaba for yourself. It is such big water, in both volume and length, that it's quickly apparent that the judge knew exactly what he was doing when he leaked the news about it. A visiting angler has as much chance of stumbling on the pool described in "Big Secret Trout" as he does coming upon Frenchman's Pond while tromping aimlessly through the endless cedar swamps and sedge meadows south of Marquette. In short, the place is safe.

The Escanaba slices north to south across the U.P.'s midsection, roughly between Marquette and Escanaba, and is paralleled much of its length by highways and county roads. In spite of those civilized encroachments, the river has

retained most of the features of more remote rivers. Immediately downstream from the town of Gwinn it slips into the kind of country the Upper Peninsula is notorious for, past sudden outcroppings of jagged, iron-colored rock, through forests lush with pine, spruce, and tamarack, and with underbrush so thick that upright creatures can pass through only with difficulty. Creeks and small rivers join the mainstream over cascading ledges, or merge slowly, darkly, from marshes of tag alders. Sometimes, if you bust your way through those tag alders, the thickets open into meadows spotted with room-sized beaver ponds. Black bears, coyotes, and eagles thrive in the region. Moose have been reintroduced and are proliferating. Wolves are occasionally reported. Certain creeks and ponds, if we are to believe Robert Traver, shelter lovely, delicate, leader-shy mermaids.

I've floated the Escanaba several times, and like trout rivers everywhere, it has proven fickle and moody. Only once did I find trout the way I dreamed I would. Craig Date and I had been canoeing and fishing the river all day, and had caught nothing but a few undersize brookies and browns. The morning had turned bright—the kiss of death on U.P. waters—and by afternoon we had given up on the fishing and just paddled, enjoying the river.

We made camp that night at an abandoned state forest campground that appeared to have hosted a few thousand Saturday-night beer parties. The campground was equipped only with a well and a hand pump with the handle broken from the shaft, an outhouse tipped over into the thimbleberry bushes, one or two broken, moldering picnic tables still chained to concrete deadmen, and garbage barrels buried beneath heaps of cans and bottles. It was too late in the day to risk trying to find another place before dark, so we set our tent on a clean grassy knoll beside the river, as far from the trashed campground as possible, built a fire, and cooked dinner.

Later we waded into the river and began casting weighted nymphs into a chest-deep run of slow water along the opposite shore. The river here was deeper than the stretch immediately upstream, where it was mostly shallow riffles flowing over clean bedrock, and downstream where it funneled into a long rapids of standing, white-tipped waves. Though it was deep and inviting, the water seemed devoid of trout, the surface still and lifeless. After sunset Craig lost interest and went to bed. It was then, with the day dwindling down to faint light, that the hatches began, several species of mayflies and caddis emerging at the same time, and suddenly there were trout rising everywhere.

It was textbook perfect: I was in good position, with the proper fly, and the trout were methodical and dazed with prosperity. Working my way slowly up the pool I cast only to the nearest risers, and steadily caught and released a half-dozen good trout. The browns ranged from twelve to fifteen inches—fat, crustacean-fed street punks—and the brook trout, ten to twelve inches, were so naive and brilliant I could not believe they inhabited the same water.

By the time darkness fell I was satiated. I waded to shore, sat on the bank to drink a warm beer, and reminded myself how fleeting success can be. Hubris may be unforgivable, but I was willing to risk it. At that moment I knew there were giant brook trout in my future.

I have yet to find them, in the U.P. or elsewhere. When that seems a significant deficiency in my character I think of John Voelker's delight at catching six- and seven-inch "troutlings" from Frenchman's Pond. Size, after all, is one of the least important qualities of brook trout.

I n the summer of 1989, Norris McDowell, then editor of *Michigan Natural Resources Magazine*, asked me if I'd like to meet John Voelker. Norris had been corresponding with Voelker for years, and always made it a point to visit him at least once each summer. Sometimes, with John's permission, he brought a friend along. That year, I was the friend.

Voelker did not know it, but our paths had already crossed. When I was a student in Marquette, I sometimes spent my study time at the library idling among the stacks, picking out books that had pleasing cover designs or intriguing titles. In those days, before the library converted to a computerized filing system, each book contained a card in a pocket inside the back cover, and on each card was written the names of those who had checked it out in the past. I began to discover, completely by accident, that an amazing number of the books I chose at random had been checked out at one time or another by John Voelker. The range of his interests astounded me. He had investigated such varied subjects as oriental philosophy, world history, the occult, semantics, theology, classic French literature, geology, paleontology, and fisheries biology. He had checked out most of the works of most of the authors I was interested in, both famous and obscure, ancient and contemporary, and had, on occasion, in the same scrawled and unmistakable handwriting of his signature, made comments in pencil in the margins, as if, while reading, he had forgotten the book he held was the library's and not his own. It became an uncanny game. Some days a quarter of the books I lifted from the shelves had John Voelker's name penned on the card in the back.

Ten years later, while we sat drinking coffee in an Ishpeming restaurant, I described to him how I once sifted through library books looking for his signature. He laughed, and admitted that scribbling notes in the margins of other people's books was "just one of many unfortunate habits."

Having heard for years about this robust man who defied age, I was a little shocked on meeting him to see a frail man who looked all of his eighty-six years. His eyes were red and moist, his nose large and as rough as if it had been chiseled from stone. His movements were deliberate, and he walked cautiously to avoid a misstep and a fall.

I soon realized I was mistaken to think of him as frail. It took only moments to become completely, unabashedly, and permanently mesmerized and to understand why television commentator Charles Kuralt, after interviewing Voelker for an "On the Road" segment, declared him the greatest man he had ever met. He had presence and charisma, the kind that fills a room.

Voelker often spent his mornings drinking coffee and playing cribbage with friends at the Rainbow Bar in Ishpeming, an aging, nondescript corner tavern that managed to stay in business without a sign to identify it. From the outside it was difficult to tell whether it was a place of business or a residence. It was still closed the morning Norris McDowell and I visited Voelker—"Pauly probably overslept," Voelker explained—so we sat in the restaurant next door and ordered coffee.

While we waited, Voelker asked where I lived, fixing me with an expression I would soon recognize as a normal baleful look of curiosity and playfulness, and said he had been to my city once to speak at a symposium about Ernest Hemingway. He had never met Hemingway, although he had long been friends with his sister Sunny, and on occasion had fished with their uncle in the Petoskey area. He could never understand, he said, why Hemingway went on to become a killer of big game and "whales" instead of remaining content with the small trout of northern Michigan. "But he was a very complex individual," he said.

While we talked, the bar opened. When we entered, Pauly, a tiny, shrunken, gray-faced old man, was wiping the bar top with a towel. He ignored us.

"Good morning, Pauly," John said in a hearty voice. He was ignored. "Pauly, do you think we might borrow your cribbage board?" Pauly gave no evidence of having heard. Winking at Norris and me, Voelker lowered himself into a booth. Pauly, in his own good time, and still without a word, placed the board on the bar top, and I fetched it and gave it to Voelker.

The Rainbow Bar was a workingman's club. It was furnished with hammered, fake marble panels on the walls, glittery molded-plastic beer advertisements, a gilt-edged mirror, and polished brass rails along the bar top—all intended to replicate wealth, Voelker explained, but at a price the work-

ing-class residents of Ishpeming could afford. A high percent-
age of those residents are descended from Scandinavian
immigrants who came to America seeking prosperity and
ease and settled in this difficult, winter-razed region near
Lake Superior because it reminded them of home. Like their
fathers and grandfathers before them, many of the working-
age men today are miners—at least those who are not among
the 15 or 20 percent who are perpetually unemployed—and
can often be seen striding tired and dirty into downtown
Ishpeming after a shift spent busting iron ore from shafts
hundreds of feet underground. They go into the half-dozen
or so bars that line the little downtown district, where they
order shots and beers, lean on the bar, and talk about hunting
and fishing. They are people John Voelker was comfortable
with all his life.

Stakes in cribbage were twenty-five cents per game, and
Voelker played with ruthless fervor. He took some pity on
me, a beginning player, by overlooking some of my errors
and pointing out combinations of cards I had missed. Each
time he won, however, he laughed gleefully and took my
quarter with a bow and a formal "I thank you, sir." With
Norris he was less solicitous. Norris had already proven himself a formidable opponent, beating John soundly during their
last meeting, thereby robbing him of the self-ordained title of
"Cribbage Champion of the Upper Peninsula," and further
humiliating him by asking John to provide him with a signed
affidavit relinquishing the crown—later framing the docu-
ment and hanging it in his office in Lansing. This morning,
however, the cards were in John's favor and he won two out
of three games, recapturing his title. He laid his winnings on
the bar and ordered a round of Cokes in tall-neck bottles. We
drank them down and left for Frenchman's Pond.

I was invited to ride in the fish car with Voelker, while
Norris followed in his own truck. I could scarcely fit inside.
John lifted books, sweaters, gloves, and a covered dish of
blueberry muffins off the passenger seat, piling them on the
heaps of debris that filled the back seat nearly to eye level.
The vehicle was the latest in a succession of fish cars, a Jeep

wagon only four years old but which had already logged nearly 170,000 miles. Virtually all those miles were driven in the central Upper Peninsula. All his life Voelker was a prodigious traveler of back roads and timber trails, a trait common in the U.P., where families often spend weekends exploring the seemingly endless network of old two-tracks. The usual practice is to load up the family car with gas, food, and beverages, pile in with the kids, take off for the woods, and get promptly lost. They drive around all day at five or ten miles per hour, discover a good berry patch or two, have a picnic, then drive on until the two-track intersects a county road and they can try to guess where the hell they are. If there's enough daylight left, they turn back into the woods and get lost again.

Voelker's fish car was loaded with anything he was likely to need while lost in the woods, plus a considerable number of wonderfully useless items. A turkey feather was stuck in the passenger-side visor. The floor was paved with a jumble of dirty bricks. In the back, forming the top layer of the multilayered heap, were a disassembled fly rod, a beat-up landing net bound with twine to a three-foot length of maple branch, three or four old wicker baskets, a rain jacket, several pairs of rubber boots and waders, two or three sweaters, a battered slouch hat ("I used to be able to order these hats from some mail-order house," Voelker explained, "but they don't make them anymore; if you find something you like in this world, young man, you'd better buy the patent"), and a small cardboard box handprinted with the message "Caution, this box contains the most deadly flies on earth."

We stopped briefly at the post office, where Voelker noticed Norris pulling into a no-parking zone, and said, "I shall come out of retirement to write 'The Anatomy of a Parking Ticket.' " Then we left town, rolling through a stop sign onto a secondary highway, and directly into the path of a speeding dump truck. The truck began veering for the shoulder even before we pulled out. As we drove past the driver leaned out and waved respectfully.

We headed north and east, driving a careful twenty-

five miles per hour on one of the U.P.'s newer highways—
straddling the white line on the side of the road, two wheels
resolved to progress, two wheels lagging on the shoulder—
and for the next hour and a half I listened to a brilliant,
nonstop monologue about the history of the region, the state
of the environment, the future of the world, the trouble with
politicians, the twin curses of airplanes and automobiles, the
heartlessness of Republicans, and the therapeutic values of
bourbon, brook trout, and wild mushrooms, all spiced with
such "fifty-cent epigrams" as, "That building looks as cheap
as a five-dollar toupee," and "Cribbage is the greatest card
game yet invented by God or man, but bridge, like the stock
market, is nothing but organized cheating." Actually, the
conversation was not a monologue so much as a mono-dia-
logue, for Voelker talked freely to himself. "It is difficult to
determine whether airplanes or automobiles were the greatest mistake," he might say. "Why is that, John?" he asked
himself. "Because airplanes opened vast regions of the earth
to plunder and overdevelopment, yet the automobile has
increased the pace of everyday life to a nearly unbearable
rate. People were once limited to the speed their horses could
run. Now they are limited only to the speeds the highways
can accommodate."

"Do you talk to yourself, young man?" he asked once,
eyes twinkling.

After a few miles we pulled off the highway and followed a two-track through high grass—"I prefer never to
drive on pavement, although it's become a necessary evil"—
and passed a devastated slope that had once been a hardwood
forest. Voelker described how the heavy equipment used to
clear-cut timber uprooted and destroyed wildflowers, blue-
berries, and ferns, leaving rolling hillsides stripped of everything but stumps and slashings. The resulting inevitable
erosion washes sand into streams and ponds, clogging the
gravel beds necessary for trout to spawn, and the loss of the
shade-giving trees causes the waters to warm so much in
some cases that trout cannot live there at all. That, and over-

fishing, has caused a serious decline in the number of native brook trout in the U.P.

"When I was a young man there were trout everywhere in this country," Voelker said. "Every puddle had its population of brook trout. You could hardly drop a bucket in a well without coming up with a trout."

Now and then we stopped to examine interesting trees, inspect deer tracks, and plunder clumps of berries. Voelker attacked sugarplum bushes the way a bear might, stripping branches with both paws, eating gleefully. Once he halted the truck abruptly and backed up so I could lean out the window and see two white birches he had described in print as entwined like lovers.

Frenchman's Pond lies at the end of four miles of what may be the most uninviting two-track road in the Upper Peninsula. The poor, rutted, washed-out, overgrown trail appears impassable, an impression Voelker cultivated with care. At various spots—say where the road made a dangerously sharp downward turn over slabs of bald bedrock—he had seeded the roadside with an assortment of battered and rusting tailpipes, mufflers, and driveshafts, the way a witch doctor might try to discourage visitors by scattering human bones along the trail to his encampment. At one time the road traveled its entire length through rolling wooded hills where Voelker was constantly distracted by the bounty of berries and mushrooms. He owned and preserved the 160 acres surrounding his camp, but was unable to protect the adjacent acreage and in the last years of his life the road to his camp passed beneath hills as naked and stubbled as poorly barbered skulls, the road churned to sand by the wheels of logging trucks. He did not accept the indignity gracefully.

At Frenchman's Pond I was introduced to Ted Bogdan, Paul Grant, and Jim Washinawatok, three friends of Voelker's who had been fishing there all morning. The camp was like any boy's ideal clubhouse. The building was small, perhaps twelve by eighteen feet, built of rough-hewn boards, with a floor of unfinished planks, a squeaking screen door, and smudged windows looking over the pond. Inside was a table just large enough to allow two people to hunker over a cribbage board. On the walls above a narrow bunk and a couch were shelves lined with fifteen or twenty empty bourbon bottles and rows of assorted memorabilia and oddities. The walls were hung with curling and water-stained calendars, posters of partially clad women, careless artwork, and framed pages from magazines. Everything was deliciously worn and dusty.

Outside, the yard was filled with what could have been the dregs of a flea market. It was cluttered with broken chairs, frail tables, peeling church pews, rusting metal wind vanes and chimes, charcoal grills, various mysterious pieces of junk, a storage shed, and an outhouse. Fly rods leaned against trees.

The pond itself is an old beaver flooding confined within the original, narrow, slowly bending streambed and lined with huckleberry thickets and spruce stands. It's a quarter-mile in length, a long cast wide most of the way, crossed in its center by a hand-hewn wooden footbridge. Much of the length of the pond the water is three to five feet deep, over a bottom of lush weeds, although there is a much deeper pool down near the old dam, along with scattered spring holes of uncertain depth. It is occupied only by brook trout, most of them troutlings measuring only four to eight inches, but there are a few larger fish. Jim Washinawatok had spent the night at the camp, and told us that the evening before he had hooked and lost a brookie that would have gone fourteen inches. Voelker did not seem surprised to hear it.

Surrounding the pond are a dozen or so small, wooden platforms spaced every fifty or one hundred feet along the marshy edges of the water. The platforms, reached by paths of muck and half-sunk boards laid end to end, allow space for a decent backcast over the marsh grasses that grow between the pond and the fringe of spruces.

We passed the morning and early afternoon playing cribbage and talking. Voelker sipped a beer or two, expressing his keen disappointment that due to doctor's orders he was prohibited from drinking his beloved old-fashioneds. He invited me to fish the pond and seemed genuinely disappointed that he did not feel well enough to join me. In half an hour of casting from a platform on the far shore I caught two five-inch trout.

When I returned to the cabin, Norris and Ted were exchanging glances. Voelker, sagging in his chair, appeared to be very tired. But even in his weariness it was evident there was no place he would rather be. He watched with bright eyes as the breeze flurried the surface of the pond, and he was quick to respond to the banter of the younger men. He said earlier that he had always refused every offer of a lucrative law career in more prosperous regions, and had after three years resigned his position on the Michigan Supreme Court, a job that required he reside in Lansing, three or four hundred miles from anyone who said, "Ya, dat's fer shore." The U.P. was where he belonged, he said. He had been very content to spend his life there.

But now it was time he returned to Ishpeming. He hoped we would all stay at the pond as long as we wished. Fish if we liked. Make ourselves at home.

We shook hands, and he drove away, his Jeep lurching up the rocky trail and out of sight. I was certain I would never see him again.

Before we left, Norris and I took a walk. We crossed the footbridge over the pond and followed a well-traveled path through the woods. It ended at the beaver dam, an ancient structure of woven silver branches anchored now with grass and living trees. The deepest water in the pond was there, a dark pool surrounded by old algae-coated sticks curving above the bottom like ribs. Sunlight glittered on the pond and we could hear water trickling through the branches of the dam into the creek below us. We wondered how many times John Voelker had walked to this very spot, his pondering heart filled with love for small trout and big country.

THE TRUMPET ON
THE DEAD

In those days in Marquette I took a lot more for granted than I do now. I did not, for instance, consider it odd that in country crossed by such rivers as the Two Hearted, Laughing Whitefish, and Yellow Dog, much of my time would be spent fishing a river named the Dead. I confronted the world then as a set of given facts, and little more. Irony was lost on me. The river was there to be fished, and I had no time for subtleties.

Like many downstaters who attend Northern Michigan University, I was there for the country. It was delightful to find a city of Marquette's size, the largest in the Upper Peninsula, with unspoiled and beautiful country literally at the city limits. Even those places that were most popular gave access to a wildness that is rarely encountered in the Lower Peninsula. A few miles from campus, at the summit of a little mountain known as Sugar Loaf, you could stand on rock outcroppings and look north over the almost frightening vastness of Lake Superior, then turn south and see unbroken hills of forest tumbling inland toward the horizon like bunched rugs. It was country—and this is what I had come north to find—big enough to get lost in.

During the first winter, when I went to the university library intending to study for my classes, I passed much of my time scanning topographical maps and searching out references to local trout streams in outdoor magazines and out-of-print books. It was during those mildly academic pursuits that I became interested in the Dead.

The river attracted me at first for mostly utilitarian reasons. Gail and I were determined to be year-round residents, not merely students who migrated south for the summers to find work in more prosperous lower Michigan. We had to find employment, which meant that I would have to take my fishing where and when I could, and the closer to home the better. In the spring I was hired by a landscaping firm that specialized in laying sod. Homeowners in Marquette demanded instant lawns—they wanted to enjoy lush green grass for those ninety or so days of mild weather each summer—forcing us to work long days "prepping" yards by raking out stones and spreading topsoil, then laying endless truckloads of transplanted Kentucky bluegrass. At the end of each workday, with only a few hours of daylight left, it was important to rush as quickly as possible to the nearest good trout water.

Because it is located so close to the city, the Dead has long been used as a source of hydroelectric power. The dams divide it into reservoirs, each separated by short stretches of free-flowing river. Most of that first summer I fished the sections immediately below the nearest dams, following wide trails lined with discarded bait containers, fishing only where it was most convenient. I did not, predictably, catch many trout.

One day near the end of the summer I drove down a

gravel road that ran parallel to a section of river I had never seen. I parked my car where power lines crossed the road, and walked to the crest of a hill overlooking a stretch of deep, slow-moving river. At midstream was a rock large enough to rise above the surface. The current trailed behind it on both sides, surrounding an eddy. As I watched, a large fish rose in the eddy, swelling the surface and pushing a wave downstream.

It turned out to be exactly what I was looking for. Flowing from one power dam to the impoundment of another was a mile of river inhabited by brook trout, browns, and rainbows. Although the little section of river was located only fifteen minutes from Marquette, I fished there dozens of times that summer and the next and never saw another angler.

Upstream from the power line were riffles and rocky pools stepping down from the dam, while in the lower half, slow, deep water snaked through tag alder marshes to the next impoundment. I would intercept the river and fish upstream into the fast water, or walk downstream, where the river became too deep to wade, following the difficult, overgrown bank and making short rollcasts to let my flies drift back against the shore. Exploring that slow water one bright afternoon I spotted a pair of brook trout, fat as bass and perhaps eighteen inches long, finning in the shadows beneath a leaning maple. I could see their white-edged fins clearly, their spots, even the hinges of their jaws working as if chewing on minute aquatic appetizers. Before I was able to back away and attempt a cast, they sensed my presence, shot into the deep water at midstream, and disappeared.

Some days I drove a half-mile farther and parked at a small turnaround where the road dead-ended. A path led through the trees, over a swinging footbridge across a slough of stagnant, oil-slicked water, then on to the power dam. If no flies were hatching I would wade downstream below the dam, casting weighted nymphs. Once, in a chute of fast water at the outside of the first bend, a rainbow as long as my forearm somersaulted from the river with my fly in its mouth. I saw it in stop-action: the pink stripe, the broad tail, the tippet wisping from its mouth. I drew up on the trout long enough to feel it throb, and it was off. A few casts later, in a chest-deep pool shaded by cedars, a fifteen-inch brown trout took the nymph, then ran, leaping like a rainbow. The next pool gave up another brown, sixteen inches long. Both were plump, healthy trout, with the vivid, brightly colored spots of wild fish. Downstream, in a small, quick run of water where the surface was as slick as a window, I stood in one spot and caught a half-dozen browns and brookies up to twelve inches.

Other days the river seemed contaminated by ennui and lassitude. Pools that had been full of trout became bleak and transparent and void of possibility. Only then would I wonder about the significance of the river's name. I would give up finally, sit on the bank, and watch the moving water so long even the trees would begin to sway and swim.

When we could get away, Gail and I used the weekends to explore other waters in the Upper Peninsula. A friend had come across a tiny makeshift shack on the Yellow Dog River, in the wild and overgrown Yellow Dog Plains northwest of Marquette, and we stayed there a few weekends to fish for brook trout. The shack was not much larger than an ice shanty, but was equipped with bunk beds and a rickety table, and had a cobbled shelf along one wall lined with an assortment of canned soups and vegetables. The owners left the door unlocked and had painted a sign on it inviting visitors to use the cabin if they wished, but to leave it in better shape than they found it, a request that was easy to honor. We caught small, brilliantly colored brook trout from the Yellow Dog, and stayed up late around the campfire watching the night sky and planning trips to rivers like the Escanaba, Ontonagon, Fox, and Two Hearted.

But I always returned to the Dead and that overlooked stretch of river near Marquette. One evening I found the slow water below the power line covered with the swirls and surges of large trout rising to a hatch of mayflies. In two casts I caught a pair of sixteen-inch browns, then a few casts later a seventeen-incher. Even while those trout thrashed on the surface and ran through the heart of the pool, other, larger fish rose to mayflies with a recklessness I have never witnessed since. I became too excited, cast wildly, hooked trees with my backcasts. Somehow I managed to make one decent cast over a large riser that was pushing wakes ahead of itself near the center of the pool. It rose to the fly and took it, but there was too much slack in my line and I could not set the hook. When, abruptly, the hatch ended, the river grew so still it could have been empty of everything but crayfish and mud puppies.

In September of our second year in Marquette, just before the beginning of the new semester at the university, Gail and I learned that we would soon be parents. At the same time, my landscaping job ended, and, in a region then suffering one of the highest unemployment rates in the U.S., there were few other opportunities available. Gail earned minimum wage clerking at a shop in Marquette's fledgling mall, and I found temporary work laying railroad track outside of Ishpeming, but it was obvious our days in Marquette were coming to an end. Gail's father offered me a job as a framing carpenter in lower Michigan and I accepted.

The last time I fished the Dead River I parked at the end of the road and followed the trail to the old swinging bridge. In the woods the maples and birches had turned color already, their leaves tipped with splashes of scarlet and yellow. Pausing on the bridge to look down into the oily slough and its border of duckweed, I could hear the effortless, humming activity of the generators in the power dam.

The river was disappointing. It was one of those days when nothing happened, when there were no insects, no fish rising, not even the eager six-inch rainbows that so often leaped and splashed at the edges of the river. A hundred feet upstream water boiled from the base of the dam. A pickup truck was parked in the little lot reserved for company vehicles beside the powerhouse. I had noticed vehicles there before, belonging, I supposed, to maintenance crews or inspectors.

I fished down through the first deep pool below the dam

and caught nothing. The water was too low and clear to hold secrets. After a dozen casts I stood in the river, my line trailing, watching and listening and thinking about the future.

That's when I heard the trumpet. Coming from inside the powerhouse at the dam were melodic, mournful, full-throated notes straight out of back-alley blues bars and 78-RPM records. Whoever the trumpeter was, he was excellent. I imagined him in green work clothes standing at the center of that busily humming building with his eyes closed, his

horn tipped back and pouring forth soulful, elegant music. It was his song, his moment, and I knew it had nothing to do with me. I was not trying to find significance in the event. It was simply something happening my last day on the Dead.

But still it haunted me. The melody was as sad and final as a dirge. It swirled downstream with the river, blending water sounds and blues notes, a strange but harmonious chording. I reeled in my line and waded to shore. The first birch leaves had fallen, fresh and yellow, and rested poised on the grass on the bank. By the time the music ended I was ready to go home.

KING TROUT

I suppose, seen from a long enough perspective, the Boardman River is of little importance. It is, after all, a small river, beginning in a conjunction of springs and creeks east of Kalkaska in northwest lower Michigan, and flowing some forty miles to Traverse City, where it ends in West Grand Traverse Bay. It is a river with an unexceptional, uninspired name, bestowed in honor of an early profiteer who hired men to cut and ship away the white pines that once grew along its banks. It is not prettier or cleaner or more exciting than hundreds of small rivers that wind across the upper Midwest.

In the greater world of rivers, the Boardman is just average, nothing special. Or maybe very special.

Leafing through a tattered, 1959 edition of *Outdoor Life*

not long ago in an antique bookshop, I was surprised to find the Boardman River described as "world famed," and listed as one of America's hundred-best trout streams. I had mixed feelings about the honor. I had visited some of North America's most famous rivers and had seen the mobs lining their banks and crowding their waters. The cost of fame was high on those rivers, and I had come home relieved to find the beautiful, neglected Boardman still beautiful and still neglected. I was proud she had been included among the top hundred rivers, but I wished the list was a little longer, say five hundred or a thousand.

There is probably little to worry about. The Boardman is not the kind of river to attract much attention. It does not have the prolific hatches or the abundant numbers of trout it takes to draw widespread notice from trout anglers. It is protected by its location, well off the Highway I-75 artery that runs up the center of the state and connects so many anglers with the north country of Michigan. Most of those anglers stop at the Au Sable, which is closer to the downstate population centers, easier to reach, and much more productive. The Au Sable, with its mainstream, North Branch, and South Branch, is an outstanding river system, big enough and rich enough to support large numbers of fishermen and still produce the best hatches and the healthiest populations of wild trout in the Midwest. It deserves all the attention it gets. And it leaves the little Boardman, which would not bear up well to fame, in a safe, nearly forgotten backwater.

In one of those closing circles you notice more as the years go by, Gail and I returned to Traverse City, to Long Lake, and again fished and canoed the waters of our childhoods. There would be more travel to come, and a two-year sojourn in Louisville, but we knew we had returned to a place we would always consider home. I began fishing the Boardman again, and that first summer I learned of an enormous brown trout living in the river, a trout I immediately thought of as the King.

A trout like that only shows up every ten years or so in the Boardman. We would always hear about him first, like a bully who's making a reputation down at the corner tavern. Nobody knows where he comes from. He seems to appear one day with his outrageous dimensions already formed, as if he had been released full-grown into the river. Somebody casts into a favorite pool, gets his line broken, and a new chapter in the folklore of the river begins.

I first heard about the King in the supermarket line at Prevo's Market, where a talkative fellow ahead of me was bragging about the giant trout he had seen in a certain not-to-be-named pool in the Boardman. He tried to be discreet, but he talked too much and I knew the place immediately: a big, deep eddy tight against the bank, where the river bends at the railroad grade not far below Garfield Road. The man said he was fishing there early one morning when some trick of the light allowed him to look down from the bank above and see in as easily as through an open window. What he saw was a brown trout so big, he said, it scared him.

Later, a friend claimed he hooked that same fish one July midnight during a hatch of *Hexagenia* mayflies. The hatch was nearly finished and most of the trout upstream and down had already gorged themselves on the giant mayflies and had ceased rising. The flies still trapped on the water were collected against the upstream sides of logs or circling in small rafts and clots in the eddies at the edges of pools. Only then did the big trout beneath the railroad grade start feeding. He sipped spent mayflies the way you would sip marshmallows from a cup of hot chocolate. My friend cast blindly in the darkness and got lucky. The battle was short, but memorable. He never saw the fish, never really had hope of landing it, but he insisted it was the largest trout he had ever hooked.

I never raised him to a fly, never even saw him. But for years afterward, whenever I fished that stretch of river I could not resist casting to the dark, strangely lifeless eddy against the bank beneath the railroad bed. There were no small trout there. Nothing seemed to live in that dark water unless it was a kind of barely perceived intelligence.

I'm not one to horde such secrets. I showed the spot to Mike McCumby, my most trusted fishing buddy, and told

him the story I had overheard. Mike and I had been drifting weighted nymphs through the pools and riffles upstream and had taken a few small trout. Along the way, in shallow water near the bank, we found the severed head of a large rainbow trout. It appeared to have been chewed off, or maybe hacked from the body with a dull hatchet. We hadn't heard of a rainbow caught in those waters in years and decided it was an omen, maybe good, maybe bad. The incident nagged at us. When we reached the railroad pool it was only natural to tell Mike about the equally nagging story I had been hearing about the King.

"I know," he said. "I've heard."

"Ever see him?"

"Nope."

We flipped a coin and Mike won. He circled ahead and entered the river carefully, wading slowly into position above and across from the pool, where he could make a short downstream cast and get a decent drift. He tied on a large weighted nymph and began working it slowly through all the water in the bend.

I sat on the bank, well downstream from the pool. At

one time, even before Mike and I were old enough to cast bobbers off docks for bluegills, this river was known around the state for its big brown trout. It was no secret: Fishermen came first to fish for its grayling, then for its brook trout, rainbows, and brown trout. It was the home water of Leonard Halladay, who in 1922 invented the Adams dry fly about a half-mile from where Mike now fished. The Adams has since become one of the most frequently used dry flies in the world, and Len Halladay one of the familiar names in the history of fly fishing. According to legend, Halladay once hooked a monstrous rainbow in this stretch of river, a trout at least three feet long that eventually wrapped around a log and broke off.

In 1920, eighteen-year-old Ernest Hemingway stopped to fish this stretch of the Boardman on his way to the Hemingway summer home on Walloon Lake. He and his pal Lew Clarahan had taken the ferry from Chicago to Frankfort and were hiking and riding trains north, fishing when the urge struck them, camping, trying their best to live off the land. The Boardman was a logical stop along the way. The grayling were gone by then, but there were brook trout, rainbows, occasional browns. It should have been an easy place to catch a meal. But they caught nothing. They fished until dark then went supperless to their open beds of spruce boughs. At 2:00 A.M. it began to rain. It rained so hard there was no hope of sleeping through it, so they got up and fished. Shortly after sunrise Clarahan caught two suckers on worms. The boys carried them to a farmhouse in Mayfield (possibly the same house Mike and his wife, Marcy, and their children live in now) and traded them to an elderly couple for a quart of milk.

Generations of locally famed anglers grew up on the Boardman. Many of them fished only with fly rods and specialized in chasing big brown trout. For years it was not uncommon for those local experts to catch trout weighing six or eight pounds.

Most of the local experts now think those giant trout are gone forever. They'll admit to the occasional twenty-incher, but they're convinced the biggest browns, the ones measured by weight rather than length, have disappeared for good. Overfishing and unwise management are usually blamed. It's commonly believed that you have to fish the Great Lakes if you want to find trout by the ton, something a lot of anglers apparently want. Fish the Boardman for the aesthetics, it's said, for the tradition. But don't expect too much.

I refused to believe it. So did Mike. He fished the pool for forty-five minutes before giving up and joining me on the bank.

"Too bright," he said. "Let's come down here about two in the morning and see if that old brown isn't cruising the flats looking for bait fish."

"Could work. He has to eat sometime."

"Sure he does. We should do that some night."

"We should."

It's easy to imagine how it might go. We would follow the trail down by flashlight until it petered out in the meadow near the apple trees, then find our way through the aspens to the low ground where the alder thickets grew. We would turn the lights off when we neared the river and stand there a moment to let our eyes adjust. The frogs and insects would be sounding off and the cool night air would be flowing downstream with the river, carrying the ripe, decaying odor of the lowlands. Upstream from the Railroad Pool we would ease into the water and begin casting big, black muddler minnows. Quartered downstream, the flies would trail tiny wakes in the moonlight. Something would be sure to happen. We might feel it first, a hesitation, a cessation. Then there would be the sudden heave of the water and a swirl. One of us, it wouldn't matter who, would raise his rod to strike, then call out in triumph while the trout made his first, long, furious run.

That's one way it could turn out. But there's no rush. Big, difficult-to-catch trout tend to live very long lives, much longer than biologists suspect. I don't know anyone in any particular hurry to catch the King, not even the friend who stung him that night during the hex hatch and who now spends more time talking about him than fishing for him.

In my own years of fishing for trout, I've never caught one like the King. I suspect such fish are reserved for special, singular moments. Maybe I've already missed mine, I don't know. But I know that catching a trout like that isn't the point. The point, of course, is believing that he's there.

Haunted By
the Hex

In Michigan your best hope of deceiving a large brown trout with an artificial fly is to fish at night, particularly during the nocturnal emergence of mayflies known as the hex hatch. Two or three weeks each summer, anyone who fishes the hatch becomes a desperate, weary, and haggard creature of the night. For trout it's an occasion for feasting and high times. For anglers obsessed with casting dry flies to large feeding trout it's the Kentucky Derby, World Series, and Super Bowl compressed into one frenetic event.

The *Hexagenia* mayfly is an absolute cheeseburger of an insect. It is so large that it brings out the glutton in even the wisest trout, an event of great importance to fly casters who must remain content, most of the season, catching trout that rarely exceed fourteen or fifteen inches in length. Just as significant is the fact that the hex hatch occurs in rivers and lakes at night, during the first two or three hours of darkness, a time when very large, very cautious trout feel secure enough to feed at the surface and will often cruise a river, gorging on insects, generally having a reckless and uninhibited good time. Anglers who have the temperament to wade blindly into rivers pocked with eight-foot holes, who are immune to swarms of mosquitoes, and who have mastered the art of casting fly lines among invisible branches have reported having a rollicking fine time themselves.

My own introduction to the pleasures and hazards of the hex came in early 1972, when I had the good fortune to meet a man named Bud Haywood, a typewriter repairman from Traverse City who was probably the most enthusiastic fisherman I have ever known. I was seventeen, quite enthusiastic myself, and began following Bud around in joyful and shameless puppy fashion. He did not seem to mind. Bud could recite dozens of elaborately detailed fishing stories and he seemed to appreciate having an audience. Some of the most fascinating of his stories involved a hatch of large bugs—he called them "caddis"—that took place every summer on the Boardman River and attracted the attention of the brown trout that lived there. He described trout of four, six, and eight pounds he had caught during the twenty or so years he had been fishing the hatch; recalled an evening when he took three six-pounders from the same pool; told of hooking and losing a fish he was convinced weighed more than ten pounds. When he mentioned in passing that I should join him sometime to fish the hatch, I leaped for a calendar, made him circle a date, did everything but draw up a contract.

Six months later, on a hot, sticky evening in early July, I stood in chest waders in the Boardman, circled by a halo of mosquitoes, watching Bud disappear around the bend upstream. Where I stood the river makes a series of lazy bends through a valley clogged with tag alders and cattail bogs. The river is not large—perhaps sixty feet wide—but it is deep and slow, with dark pools at each bend dropping away to cathedral-like depths. In my fevered state those depths seemed radiant with possibilities. I was certain dozens of muscle-bound brown trout were suspended there, waiting for darkness and the coming feeding frenzy.

The problem was, the day refused to end. The sun appeared to have gotten tangled in something just beyond the edge of the earth, locking the sky in permanent twilight. I had tied one of Bud's enormous deer-hair-and-feather dry flies to a leader cut back, at his suggestion, to six feet long and testing ten pounds in strength. It seemed as sturdy as a hawser, and certainly stout enough to horse in any trout. To pass the time I practiced false-casting, flinching each time the large fly hurtled past my head.

I was surprised, at one point, to notice the sky had produced stars. They were poor specimens, pale and weak, but sign nonetheless that night might finally come. Two events then occurred simultaneously: The river, reflecting the last light of the day, became covered with the rings and dimples of emerging mayfly duns, and the air above me filled with a buzzing sound, a droning hum like airborne electricity.

The humming sound was made by the wings of thousands of mayflies flowing upstream in a dense cloud. A flash of my pocket light caught them in stop-action: the insects larger than I had expected, graceful, their wings frozen in position. They looked like Disney creations, an army of fairies massed for an assault on an evil castle. A square yard of sky contained hundreds of them. They beat along upstream, twenty feet or so above the river, driven by their urge to propagate.

Twenty feet away, a fish rose with an abrupt slurp. It was louder and more assured than any rise I had encountered in daylight. It came again—quick, controlled, almost dainty. A trout with table manners. I estimated it to be fourteen inches long, a nice fish, a good size to warm up on before hauling in a few eight-pounders.

False-casting to lengthen line, guessing at distance and location, I placed a cast above the trout's position. There was a moment of silence while the fly drifted with the current. When the slurping rise came again I lifted my rod sharply to set the hook. I had a moment of satisfaction, even smugness. It all seemed ridiculously easy. Then the line hanging from my left hand was torn away and went rattling off through the rod guides. It slammed to a hard stop when a loop went around the seat of the reel. Something similar could happen if you were casting from a bridge and your backcast hooked the bumper of a passing Oldsmobile. My rod yanked to a flat and very unnatural position, like a palm tree in a hurricane. I hollered. The leader broke.

Hexagenia limbata. You're excused if you mispronounce it. Say hex, or giant Michigan mayfly, or the misnomer Michigan caddis, and every fly fisherman in the Midwest—and many in North America—will know exactly what you mean. Family, Ephemeridae; genus, *Hexagenia*; species, *limbata*. The largest mayfly on the continent, and so abundant in some Michigan waters that it's been found in the larval stage in concentrations of five hundred per square foot of bottom. Although the mayfly resides in clean, cool rivers and lakes throughout the Midwest, and as far east as upstate Connecticut, Michigan is at the heart of its range and probably supports the most abundant populations. The insect thrives in such fine Michigan trout rivers as the Au Sable, Manistee, Pere Marquette, White, Boardman, Jordan, Pigeon, and Black.

Like each of the more than two thousand species of mayflies in the world, *Hexagenia limbata* begins its life as a larval nymph. In the Midwest, *Hexagenia* nymphs are commonly known as "wigglers," are used as bait by fishermen, and are seined from the silt bottoms of rivers and lakes where they live in tiny U-shaped burrows. Feeding on a diet of microorganisms filtered from the water through their gills, they grow rapidly, undergoing as many as thirty molts of their skin to accommodate growth. By the summer of their first or second year they're ready for the great adventure of their lives.

In Michigan that adventure—the transformation from nymphs to winged adults—occurs usually between June 15 and July 15, varying somewhat according to location and weather. Typically, a warm, humid night in late June will trigger a hatch. It begins as darkness falls, with the nymphs leaving their burrows and swimming rapidly toward the surface. As they struggle to break free from the water they split their nymphal skins and undergo the transformation into subimagos, or duns.

The transformation is dramatic, as startling as a caterpillar's metamorphosis into a butterfly. The dun's wings are large and prominent, as tall as the insect is long, slightly opaque, and a smoky, olive color. The tail is long and arches gracefully, ending in three delicate fibers. Everything about the insect is beautiful and fragile. Try lifting one carelessly and the wings collapse in your fingers. Splash one and it becomes trapped in the surface film of the water, unable to escape.

Once the dun is fully emerged from the nymphal skin it rides the water for a few moments to dry its wings, then flies off quickly to find shelter in trees and bushes. Every stage of the process has its perils. From the moment the nymph scurries from its burrow until it flies from the water, fish are pursuing it. Once airborne it must fly a gauntlet of swallows, nighthawks, bats, and kingbirds, then find haven under bushes and tree branches where it can avoid spiders, frogs, toads, snakes, and any number of creatures looking for an easy meal.

During the next twenty-four to seventy-two hours, while hiding along shore, the duns go through yet another transformation. The changes now are more subtle. The wings lose their color, becoming nearly transparent, and the tail lengthens and spreads its three filaments as the sexual organs mature. At this stage the insect is known as an imago, or spinner. When mature, and usually after dark, the spinners leave their hiding places and gather over the water in a mating swarm, which moves in a mass upstream, near treetop level, and often includes so many insects they appear as dense as a cloud. Mating occurs over the water, during flight. Each female then drops to the surface, dips her tail in the water, and releases up to three thousand fertilized eggs. The eggs sink to the bottom, settling among stones and in protected crannies where they remain about two weeks before hatching.

Within minutes of mating, both males and females collapse spent to the water, wings outstretched, and die. It is then that they make the easiest meal, and seem most irresistible to trout. During a heavy spinner fall a river's entire population of trout will often seem to be feeding.

The hex mayfly performs two valuable functions that are not often mentioned. The first is to act as an environmental indicator. Because mayflies cannot tolerate filthy water, they are often the first warning that things are not right in a body of water. Lake Erie provides the classic example of that. *Hexagenia* once hatched in such numbers along the southern shoreline of the lake that nearby residents became accustomed to shoveling piles of dead mayflies from sidewalks and driveways in the mornings after a hatch. There were even reports of snowplows called into service to clear bug-slicked roads. In the 1940s and 1950s the hatch reached outlandish proportions, the result of the increasing organic enrichment of the water. That population explosion was short-lived however, for when the enrichment became excessive the water was unable to maintain enough oxygen to support mayfly life, and the hatches, almost from one year to the next, ceased. It took two decades of pollution control before the lake became healthy enough to support the insects again.

The other function the mayflies perform is to demonstrate that a river often contains much healthier populations of trout than daytime observers might guess. There are stretches of nearly every river, including such outstanding trout streams as the Au Sable and Manistee, that can seem as barren and lifeless as swimming pools. After a sunny afternoon of fishing transparent water apparently inhabited by nothing but crayfish and two-inch shiners, you would swear the river is devoid of game fish. A good hatch of *Hexagenia* is likely to change that opinion. The trout seem to be everywhere: along grassy cutbanks, behind half-submerged logs, in the shadows beneath cedar sweepers. Even when you catch nothing you will go home late at night tired and soggy and terrifically heartened by the activity you have witnessed.

In the years since that night when Bud Haywood introduced me to my first hex hatch, I've noticed, through a fair number of trials and a great number of errors, that it's possible to judge the approximate size of a trout by the sound it makes when feeding. The sudden splashy rises are usually made by trout under a foot long. Add some volume to the splash—a touch of alto saxophone with the clarinets—and the trout are pubescent twelve-to-fourteen inchers. Hear a deep "glub" or a weighty splash—two oboes and a tuba—and they are reckless fourteen-to-eighteen-inchers. If the rise is a wallow, a swirl, and suck, or a roiling splash that sends waves to both shores—oboes, tubas, a kettle drum, and the cello section— you may be hearing a twenty-incher. Trout larger than that avoid throwing their weight around, preferring to feed surreptitiously. They often sound something like a child sucking the last of a root-beer float through a straw. Find a regular riser that sips, slurps, or pushes waves lapping to the banks and you'd better stake a claim to it. Come early, night after night, and take up a position beside the pool where you found it—not a bad strategy if you have the patience of a monk and are disciplined enough to ignore the noisy smaller trout that are likely to be rising all around you.

That is not to say the fishing is easy. It most emphatically is not. Even at night trout want nothing to do with a sloppy cast or a fly pattern that isn't close to the size and contours of the natural mayflies they're feeding on. There's also the problem created by the sheer abundance of the mayflies. During a heavy hatch—appropriately called a blanket hatch—so many mayflies are on the water that there is little chance a trout will select the one artificial fly in the midst of all those insects. Some anglers increase their odds by counting the seconds between a regular feeder's rises, then timing their casts to coincide with it. If a large fish is hooked the battle is decidedly one-sided. The angler has the element of surprise on his side, is using relatively stout equipment, and has the benefit (theoretically) of superior intelligence. But the trout knows the terrain and knows how to use the darkness, current, snags, logs, and branches to its advantage. Far more fish are lost than landed.

O n one of those summer evenings when time comes to a quiet stop, the sun suspended low in the sky, the wind dying away like a last breath, I sat on the porch listening to a ball game on the radio—the Royals were beating the Tigers by a bunch—and watching a glass of iced tea sweat rings on the patio table. The phone rang. It was Bob Summers. "The hex hatch is on," he said. A friend of his had found rising trout the night before on the Manistee above the CCC Bridge, which meant there should be a good hatch tonight at a spot Bob knew on another river. "Let's go," he said. "Now."

Bob Summers is not a man to be put off. He's something of a legend among fly fishermen, at least among that diminishing breed of purists who still fish with split-bamboo rods. Summers grew up in Detroit, where as a teenager he one day wandered into the shop of world-famed rod maker Paul Young and was hired to clean up and do odd jobs. In time he was apprenticed to the master and learned to build rods the old-fashioned way: by hand and with supreme attention to detail.

Now Summers earns his living building fly rods that cost more than most of the used cars I've purchased in the past two decades, and he has spent a considerable amount of time fishing for trout in some of the most exotic rivers and lakes in the world. He is a busy man and when he invites you to go fishing you don't mince around with excuses like ball games and iced tea. You drop what you're doing and go.

"This place remains secret, understand?" he said, the moment I climbed into his car. I understood. Mike McCumby was there too, grinning. "I can't guarantee we'll get into any big trout," Bob went on, "but there's a good chance of it. The river's small, with lots of deep holes and undercut banks, and it flows into a lake. Big browns sometimes migrate upstream from the lake to feed on the mayflies."

We were on the river by dusk, the sun already a pastel smear on the horizon. In a few minutes the river downstream, where the last of the daylight shimmered, became covered with tiny rings, as if from a light shower of rain. Occasionally it was possible to see a delicate, perfectly formed mayfly sprout from the exact center of a ring, ride the surface for a moment, and lift soundlessly into the air. Then the spinners appeared, swarming upstream in an undulating cloud, twenty to thirty feet above the river. As they passed, individual mayflies spiraled to the water and settled with their wings spread.

Trout began rising behind every log, in every pool more than thigh deep. By now it was too dark to see rising fish, but splashes and slurps were audible up and down the river. Mike and I stood by while Bob cast to what sounded like a decent fish; he cursed extravagantly when he lifted his line to backcast at the precise moment the trout took his fly, bumping it on the nose and sending it rushing downstream. He changed positions and began casting to another riser.

Mike thought there was a large trout rising behind a stump at the edge of the current. It slurped noisily at mayflies.

"Sounds like a big trout there, Bob. Can you put a fly over him?"

"That's no trout. Has to be a frog or an otter or something, slurping like that."

"That's a trout," Mike said. He explained he had once cast to an identical sound and hooked a brown that measured just under twenty-one inches.

"I don't believe it," Bob said. He's a man with strong opinions—good company as long as you don't contradict him or get him started on such subjects as political corruption and the welfare system. "I never caught a trout that slurped like that. Must be a big toad."

Mike lengthened line and cast, but it was useless effort. Whatever was feeding behind the stump was almost impossible to reach, sheltered by overhanging branches and a snarl of logs. "That's a trout," he said, trying to send the last salvo.

"No it ain't," Bob said.

It turned into one of those nights when everything goes wrong. Fish that rose to our flies bumped them but weren't hooked, or were hooked but broke the leader, or pulled free, or, like trained porpoises, leaped cleanly over half-submerged logs and broke off. Bob, not the most patient of anglers, raged in frustration.

Late, past midnight, the hatch ended. We sprayed our flashlights across the surface of the river and saw only a few stragglers, spent-wing and waterlogged. The trout had stopped feeding.

As we waded downstream back to the car, a fish rose under the branches along the bank. We stopped and listened. It rose again, making a noise like a tuba. "Big one, cruising after stragglers," Bob said. "Try for him."

I lengthened line, guessing at distances, and cast sidearm into the dark space beneath the branches. It was like a cavern under there, too dark to see anything. Nothing happened. I waited until my line floated away from the branches, lifted it, and shot a cast deeper into the cavern. The fly drifted silently, invisible in the darkness, and suddenly, somewhere out of sight near the bank, the trout slurped, heaving the water, and I set the hook.

The fish went deep, throbbing heavily, then ran thirty feet downstream into the open river. It came out of the water in an end-over-end leap, visible in silhouette against the river. There, in midair, the hook pulled free. When we examined the fly with a flashlight the point of the barb was curled over as if it had nicked a rock on the backcast.

Mike laughed. Bob shook his head in disgust. They waded on ahead while I stood there, still rattled by the size of the trout I had lost.

One of the odd things about the hex hatch is it causes you to undergo a kind of metamorphosis yourself. For two weeks you live for the night, passing your days in a trance, haunted by the thought of trout so large you suspect you'll never land them. Then you go out on the river and prove your suspicions correct.

THE DEMISE OF
THE MICHIGAN
GRAYLING

Early in the morning, on certain stretches of the Au Sable River, you can imagine northern Michigan has changed very little over the centuries. The river is alive and clean, and flows over the same sand bottom French fur traders noticed two hundred years ago, when they first began calling it "River of Sand." Along the banks cedars have fallen into the river, creating the "sweepers" early travelers were forced to portage around or cut through, and which are used so well by trout and other fish for cover. The only sounds are the water, gurgling and whispering, and the wind in the trees on the ridge above the river.

But of course much has changed. The most significant changes began in the middle of the nineteenth century when timber cruisers found enormous stands of white pine in the area and claimed them for the lumber companies. They were soon followed by lumbermen who set up temporary camps along the river and went to work.

In the space of a few decades the land was altered entirely. The timber industry, spurred by the insistent demand for lumber from fast-growing midwestern cities like Detroit and Chicago, was incredibly profitable. According to one estimate, the lumber harvested in Michigan during the second half of the nineteenth century was worth at least a billion dollars more than all the gold dug in California in those same years. Each spring, massive log drives filled every sizable river in the northern two-thirds of the Lower Peninsula and the Upper Peninsula. From 1867 to 1883, 1.33 billion log-feet of timber was driven down the Au Sable alone. In 1890, the peak year, that river carried more than 300 million log-feet of the big pines. Within a few years, forests that had been considered an inexhaustible resource were gone, and the lumbermen moved on.

It had always been assumed that once the forests were cleared, the land in northern Michigan would be as rich as the prosperous farmlands of southern Michigan. Civil War veterans, recent immigrants, and thousands of settlers eager to make a fresh start were lured to the north by promises of cheap, fertile land. But by 1890 it was apparent that the loose, sandy soil was suited for growing pines and little else, and most farmers had already abandoned their homesteads and moved south. Those who stayed were forced to find other means of employment.

Hunting and fishing offered just that opportunity. A man named I. F. Babbitt, who came to Grayling in 1873 to survey for the Jackson, Lansing and Saginaw Railroad, settled in the area and established the first fishing camp on the Au Sable, providing visiting anglers with boats, tents, guides, and meals. Soon others followed his lead, and the region at last had an industry to replace its failing sawmills.

On the surface, at least, the river itself did not change. Log drives had scoured the bottom and left some sections choked with silt, and enough of the sweepers and logjams were cleared to allow fishermen to float the length of the river in flat-bottomed wooden boats, but the river remained essentially the same. Flowing clear and cold for 115 miles from Grayling to Oscoda, where it emptied into Lake Huron, it was a river so fine and lovely it was thought to possess powers of rejuvenation. Most important, it was filled with incredible numbers of a small, little-known fish that came to be known as the Michigan grayling.

Thaddeus Norris, a popular outdoor writer of the late nineteenth century, made several trips to northern Michigan to fish on the Au Sable, Manistee, and other rivers. At the time of his visits very little was known about the grayling found in many of those waters. In an article published in *Scribner's Monthly* in 1879 (and reprinted in *The Old Au Sable*, by Hazen L. Miller, W. B. Eerdmans Publishing Co., 1963) he wrote about the early mysteries surrounding the unusual fish:

> *It was supposed that, except in the arctic regions, [the grayling] did not exist on our continent. About ten years ago, however, hunters and those who were looking up timber lands began to talk of a white-meated fish with all the game qualities of the trout, which they captured in streams of both water-sheds—east and west—as an addition to their venison and "hard tack." It was known to them as the "white trout," the "Crawford County trout," and under other local names until a specimen in alcohol was sent to Professor E. D. Cope, of the Philadelphia Academy of Natural Sciences, who described it in the proceedings of that institution in the year 1865, and gave it the scientific name of* Thymallus tricolor, *the generic name arising from the fresh thyme-y smell of the fish when first taken from the water, the specific appellation having reference to its beautiful dorsal fin. And yet its discovery as a true grayling escaped the notice of nearly all of our fly-fishers; and to the few who might have meditated an expedition in search of it, its habitat was far off and then almost inaccessible.*

It was not long before the region became more easily accessible. When the Jackson, Lansing and Saginaw Railroad reached Grayling in the late 1870s it was used primarily to transport freshly cut pine logs south to the sawmills in Saginaw. Soon, however, the railroad began advertising hunting and fishing trips to the Grayling area, luring increasing numbers of sportsmen to the game and fish available in the newly opened region.

The word spread quickly. By the 1880s the Au Sable was gaining world fame for its grayling fishery, and was frequently visited by wealthy sportsmen from Detroit, Cleveland, Cincinnati, Buffalo, Toledo, Indianapolis, and Chicago, and occasionally from as far away as England.

Ansell Judd Northrup, a lawyer from Syracuse, New York, described the Michigan grayling in his book *Camps and Tramps in the Adirondacks, and Grayling Fishing in Northern Michigan*, published in 1880:

> *The appearance of the grayling in the water, when hooked and excited and struggling, is something beautiful to see,—the large dorsal fin being the most conspicuous and noticeable feature. The colors of both the dorsal and pectoral fins are rich and delicate beyond description,— the violet, pearly and golden tints and rainbow hues, marvelously contrasted and blended. The back is dark olive-brown; the sides and belly, silvery; the body, slim and graceful; the head small, mouth of medium size and tender; tail, forked and broad; and the adipose fin shows his royal lineage.*

The fishing for this appealing game fish was spectacular. Anglers who floated the Au Sable routinely reported catches of hundreds of grayling a day. Similar success came on such rivers as the Manistee, Jordan (one of the few Lower Peninsula rivers to be inhabited at the time by both grayling and native brook trout), the Boardman, the Pere Marquette, and the Rifle. The fish were so abundant in those waters, and so eager to take artificial flies, that it was not unusual to cast a single trace of three flies—arranged with a "trailer," and one or two "droppers" spaced along the leader—and hook several fish simultaneously. Veterans of the sport learned to allow a hooked grayling to dart around in the current until another fish grabbed the trailer fly. Fishermen hauled the grayling into their boats as fast as they could hook them, depositing them in live-boxes built into the hulls.

Standard fly-fishing equipment of the day, as described by Thaddeus Norris, included a twelve-foot rod, an eight-foot leader, and flies tied on hook sizes 7 through 10. Choice of flies was apparently a matter of personal preference, since the grayling were not particular, but Norris found "most of the flies used on Pennsylvania streams effective, and one can scarcely go amiss in his selection." He preferred using a professor for the trailer, a silver widow for the first dropper, and a white-winged coachman for the second dropper.

In his *Scribner's* article, Norris described the fishing he found during his first visit to the Au Sable, in August 1874:

> On our second day we killed and salted down—heads and tails off—a hundred and twenty pounds of fish, besides eating all we wanted. In one hanging rift close by the bank . . . I took at five casts fifteen fish, averaging three-quarters of a pound each. The following day we fished along leisurely until we had our live-boxes, containing each sixty pounds, so full that the fish began to die . . . Then we passed over splendid pools in which we could see large schools of grayling on the bottom without casting a fly; for we would not destroy them in mere wantonness.

Norris's reluctance to indulge in mere wantonness did not prevent him from making a big killing on the Manistee River in 1875, keeping more than five hundred pounds of grayling and shipping them by railroad to paying markets in Bay City and Detroit. Similar commercial ventures were a major problem on the grayling rivers. One resident recalled years later that he and his father kept a Chicago restaurant supplied with grayling from 1875 to 1881, for which they were paid the "unheard of" price of twenty-five cents per pound. Even many anglers with no interest in commercial profit could not resist exploiting the abundant and easily caught grayling. Two parties of Chicago fishermen were said to have camped on an unnamed northern river where they killed a total of eight thousand grayling, leaving many of them to rot on the banks.

A few observers had the foresight to realize the bounty could not last forever, but conservation efforts, when they came, were a case of too little and too late. Commercial sale of grayling was prohibited as early as 1875, and in 1881 a six-inch size limit was placed on the grayling, but neither law seems to have been enforced.

During the closing decade of the nineteenth century it was evident that the grayling would soon disappear. The State Board of Conservation made several clumsy efforts to save them, including transplanting fifteen hundred grayling to warm southern Michigan streams where they promptly died. All attempts to propagate the native grayling in fish hatcheries failed. Meanwhile, professional guides, concerned about their future livelihood, introduced brook, brown, and rainbow trout into the Au Sable and other former grayling rivers. The trout thrived.

Grayling were gone from the Au Sable by 1890. Within a few years an overlooked population in the upper Manistee River had been eradicated. Before the turn of the century they had disappeared from every river and stream in the Lower Peninsula.

In 1880, Ansell Judd Northrup observed that the Michigan grayling was almost certain to be doomed. "He is a simple, unsophisticated fish," he wrote, ". . . a 'free biter,' bound to disappear before the multitude of rods waved over his devoted head. The sport he affords in his capture, the taste he gratifies in the frying-pan, and the allurements of the charming streams he inhabits, all conspire with his simplicity to destroy him. Could he but learn wisdom from his crimson-spotted cousin, and would the sportsman have pity on this beautiful and gentle creature of the smoothly gliding rivers, he would long live to wave the banner of beauty and glory in the cold, clear streams of the north. But that cannot be."

The final hideout for the Michigan grayling was the Otter River, near the base of the Keweenaw Peninsula in the western Upper Peninsula. According to *Trout Streams of Michigan*, a collection of biologists' reports edited by Tom Huggler and published by the Michigan United Conservation Clubs, a lifelong resident of the Otter River region named Walter Erickson caught and released an eleven-inch grayling in the north branch of the Otter in the summer of 1934. It may have been the last Michigan grayling. Erickson caught and released that same fish several times that summer. Finally, late in the season, he caught it for the final time, slipped it into his creel, and took it home to show his children.

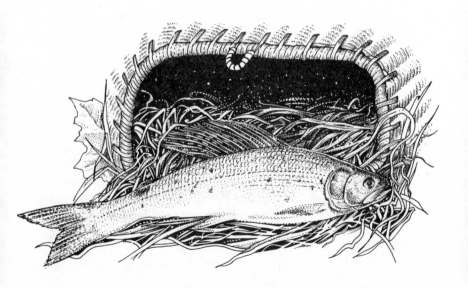

OFF-SEASON ON THE
MANISTEE

There are no grayling in Michigan rivers now, but you can find reminders of them. The cedar sweepers Thaddeus Norris described a century ago still bend to the water on most northern Michigan rivers, and the clear pools once occupied by grayling are now occupied by descendants of brook, brown, and rainbow trout planted by early fishing guides. If you know where to look, the history of the land is written all over the rivers. The history is especially rich on the Manistee.

I have never been particularly fond of the lower Manistee River. Below Tippy Dam, it is one of Michigan's most popular steelhead and salmon rivers, crowded every spring and fall with hundreds of anglers hoping to hook fish that are large, furious, and lake-fed. It's a busy place, milling with people, roiled by high water.

But my old Traverse City neighbor and friend Barry Barto, a high-school biology teacher and amateur naturalist, insisted that the lower Manistee is one of his favorite places to canoe and watch wildlife. In summer, he said, it was a different river altogether. It is low, quiet, and forgotten then, the parking lots at the public access sites are empty, the banks are grown up with osiers and tag alders that hide the deeply etched trails along the shore. I thought I knew the river fairly well, but I was wrong. In the off-season it proved to have another personality altogether.

We canoed it one weekend in June, and as far as I could tell we had the entire river to ourselves. Equipped with sandwiches, bug repellent, extra clothing, and Barry's ever-present Peterson Field Guides, we launched a canoe at the access site below Tippy Dam and immediately paddled through riffles that during the spring steelhead run were rapids, and past willow-capped islands that would be submerged when the water was high. Pools that had in spring seemed treacherous to a cautiously wading angler are shallow and transparent in summer. The banks are high, sandbars reach most of the way across the river, and ancient logs and stumps are exposed along the shore.

Those logs and stumps are remnants of nineteenth-century log drives that made the Manistee famous in a state already famous for its logging industry. By 1897 loggers in Michigan had harvested an estimated 160 billion board feet of white pine, representing about a billion trees. Some of the finest of those trees came from northern Michigan territory drained by the Manistee River. The tallest and straightest of the pines, free of knots and buoyant enough to float high and easily during the spring log drives, were known as "cork pine" and were much in demand.

The size and strength of the Manistee gave it a reputation for danger among the shanty boys and river hogs who worked it. *Michigan Log Marks*, a book compiled by the Work

Projects Administration and published by the Michigan Agricultural Experiment Station in the early 1940s, describes an early logjam on the Manistee: ". . . logs began piling up on the outer margin of the turn, driven hard into the bank by the impacts of the logs following. Soon the drive jammed the river from bank to bank, pushed by the strong current, until logs were hung up to a height of 40 feet and stopped for more than a mile upriver."

A crew was assembled to break the jam. They attacked the jumbled logs with pikes and axes, always alert for a key log that when moved might release the entire jam. When the jam finally broke free, churned by the force of tons of backed-up water, three men were caught in the tumbling logs and killed.

Evidence of those awesome logjams is still visible on the Manistee. Sand and clay banks at the river's bends are in continuous erosion, frequently unearthing hundred-year-old logs in remarkably good condition. On many of them the old "log marks" are plainly visible. Those marks, like brands on cattle, were used to identify the owners of the millions of logs that floated down the river during the spring floods. They were driven into both ends of the freshly cut timber by a laborer wielding a cast-iron hammer with raised letters or symbols on its face.

Michigan Log Marks reports that there were 339 end marks plus 258 bark marks (which were driven into the bark on the sides of the logs, rather than the ends) registered on the Manistee from 1872 to 1914, each representing a logging company with a claim on the timber stands upriver. Once the mingled logs reached Manistee Lake, they were sorted, then towed in enormous booms to sawmills on the shore.

Today, well-preserved logs along the Manistee still reveal their marks: the three interlocking circles of the Seymour Brothers, the "Triangle K" of C. F. Ruggles, the "17V" of O. P. Pillsbury, the simple square of Peters' Lumber Company, the "heart" of Ella J. Hart. Souvenir hunters have used chain saws to hack the ends off many of the most easily reached logs. Not until high water has dredged the banks, leaving them raw and exposed after the water subsides, are enough fresh logs unearthed to give you a good look at them.

A modest run of summer steelhead attracts a few anglers to the lower Manistee early on July mornings, but generally the summer fishing, what little is done, is for warm-water species. Some walleye can be found in the deepest pools and occasionally at night in the turbulent water directly below Tippy Dam. Pike, muskie, and catfish are sometimes taken. In a pool where the autumn before I had caught a lovely, fresh-run steelhead, Barry and I saw small bass and suckers finning in plain sight on bottom. Near shore a twenty-inch pike rested as still as a sunken limb, waiting for frogs or bait fish to grow careless and wander near.

We stopped for lunch at a grassy bank a mile or two below High Bridge. I learned long ago not to be in a hurry with Barry. He's distracted by every bird and every animal track, by unusual insects and blossoming wildflowers. Already we had spent as much time out of the canoe as in it, examining the logger's marks on the old logs, making forays into the woods or the willow thickets of small islands and

gravel points. He showed me sassafras trees—identified by the odd-numbered lobes on their leaves—and demonstrated how to pull up the roots of the tender saplings and strip them to make a boiled root-beer tea. He spotted kinglets, finches, and other small songbirds I would have dismissed as LBJs—Little Brown Jobs. At one point we came upon a fawn curled up perfectly still in a sun-spotted patch of grass in the woods. Not wanting to frighten it, we backed off, then froze when we heard the sudden alarmed snorting of the mother somewhere nearby in the woods. The fawn stayed put, not even twitching an ear.

A small tributary wound through fallen trees and entered the river near the spot where we stopped to eat lunch. Rather than waste time eating, Barry went off immediately to explore game trails that meandered along the riverbank. I walked over to look at the creek. When I leaned from the bank I spooked three good-sized smallmouth bass that had been hovering in the cool creek water at the confluence with the river. They swam out and took cover beside an enormous drowned log that had probably entered the river before the invention of aircraft and gas-engine automobiles, that might have floated over schools of Michigan grayling finning in the river far upstream. It seemed a perfect image: the past and the present fused, the river a living connection between them.

WINTER'S RIVER

I f you love rivers you find reasons to be near them. Winter is a good enough reason. In winter even rivers you have known all your life seem new. Get in a canoe and float downstream past the first bend and for all you know you could be riding water on another continent. It's just what the doctor ordered for seasonal affective disorder, income-tax jitters, and existential dread, and people who try it tend to get enthusiastic.

Bill Edmonson was so enthusiastic that by ten o'clock on a February morning on the Pere Marquette River he broke his second canoe paddle of the day. Like the first, it sheered off where the blade met the handle. Also like the first, Bill held the handle up in the air and looked at it with astonishment, the way he might have looked if he had dipped it into the water and something bit it off. Bill's a big guy; he doesn't know his own strength. His exertions broke two good paddles that morning and we had no more spares.

In his easy-going way—nonchalant, never riled, a southern good-old-boy raised by an accident of history in the north—Bill addressed Mark Wilkes, his partner in the bow. "Looks like you're gonna have to do all the work from now on."

Mark shrugged, adding the item to a growing list of life's injustices.

"Another day in the salt mines," he said.

Here in Michigan the sight of a canoe strapped to an automobile in January or February draws a fair amount of attention. For years my friends and I have been considered mildly deranged for doing it, a judgment we once encouraged because it gave us convenient license for further extremities of behavior. It still pleases us to pull into a restaurant parking lot on a cold, snowy morning and park our canoe-topped trucks next to vehicles loaded with skis and snowmobiles. The waitresses always ask in a wonderful, wide-eyed way if we are actually going *canoeing*.

We were college friends and friends of college friends, who came together to canoe and camp one weekend every winter. At first, while we were in our early twenties, we pretended the winter expeditions were macho initiation rites. The rivers we paddled were scenic and free-spirited and passed through nice country, but we were interested primarily in having a roaring good time and exposing ourselves to hardships severe enough to challenge our powers of endurance. In later years we would come to appreciate the trips for more subtle reasons.

The Pere Marquette, or the P.M. as nearly everyone in Michigan knows her, has always been a particular favorite among our little group. I got off to a shaky start in the relationship in 1975, during my first winter trip, when Mike

McCumby and I ended up walking out of the woods carrying nothing but the rapidly freezing clothes on our backs. We had tried to back-paddle a heavily loaded canoe away from a fallen tree, were caught sideways in conflicting currents, and capsized. For months, our friends were extremely helpful. They pointed out that the mishap was the result of our own stupidity in attempting to canoe the river during freakishly high water, for going alone, and for attempting a tricky back-paddling maneuver without the experience to do it right. It did not, they insisted, prove anything was inherently wrong with winter canoeing. Mike took the criticism well and was back on the P.M. the following winter. I spent a few years thinking about it.

Naturally, I thought primarily about all the fun I was missing. A few minutes on a northern river in winter is enough to convince you that canoeing should indeed be a year-round sport. In winter, rivers are different, their character altered by banks of sculpted ice, by barren trees, by countryside that has been largely abandoned to the snow. Paddling then becomes a process of rediscovering the rivers and the landscape, and of discovering again the sensual pleasures of gliding through clean water in a canoe. You feel the air, cold and harsh, so brittle it seems to shatter as you pass. You might turn to watch your breath fogging in the air and see a pie of snow fall from a hemlock on the bank. Once you begin noticing such things it's difficult to stop. You see ice grown into minute, precisely detailed sculptures where the water touches a trailing branch, and notice the soundless obliteration of snowflakes as they enter the river. You hear the trickle of runoff beneath the snow alongshore, the hissing of current against fringe ice, the distant thumping of a pileated woodpecker. The river breathes and whispers, blending with the thin sounds of the canoe brushing against water and slush, with the dripping of a still-held paddle. A half-hour of this and you're eager to make extravagant claims for the virtues of wilderness, even a wilderness only a few bends concealed from highways and houses.

For ten years most of us in our group tried never to miss

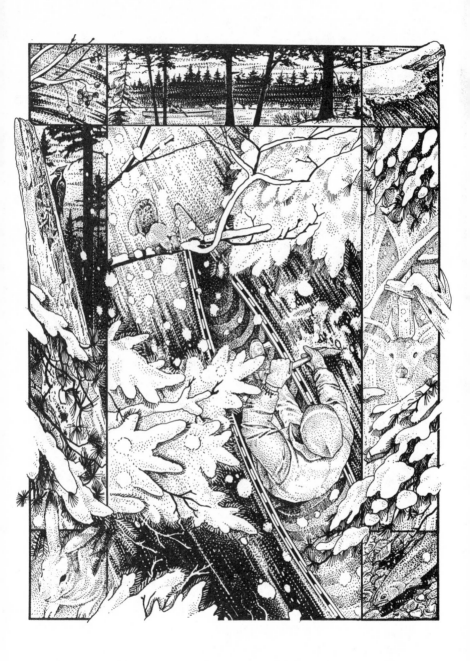

the annual winter canoe trip. But in our thirties we began skipping years. Children, jobs, and the usual responsibilities began to interfere. First a few, then all of us had excuses to miss the trip one winter, then the next, then the next. Paul Schulte, one of the original organizers, moved to Florida, where he spent his winters paddling in canals and casting for bass. Craig Date became a long-distance truck driver—it satisfied a certain restlessness—and made his home in Houston. The rest of us also scattered and began altering our priorities. When we saw each other or got the urge for late-night telephone calls, we always asked about the winter canoe trip. "Next year," we would say. Somehow, five years passed before we got together again.

The first day of this reunion weekend we stopped early, in plenty of time to set up camp and have supper cooking before darkness. Still, by the time we raised the tents, collected firewood, unpacked cook kits and food, and skewered damp boots on sticks, it was past sunset and the woods were lit with that cold blue light peculiar to winter evenings. The temperature began dropping fast and no one needed to coax Bill Edmonson—by common consent, keeper of the fire—to build one of his signature bonfires, one large enough to roast our faces so thoroughly we were grateful for our cold backsides. We sat up late around the fire, as we always do, watching sparks spiral upward to blend with stars so bright they seemed within reach.

In the morning, after a night during which none of us ever got warm, not even in state-of-the-art sleeping bags rated for near-arctic conditions, we woke to teeth-aching, breath-stopping cold. We weren't warmed even after hot coffee and a breakfast of steaming oatmeal that went from searing to tepid in the amount of time required to lift a spoonful from bowl to mouth. While breakfast cooked, Craig, his breath spouting clouds, warmed himself by performing jumping jacks. In his multiple layers of bulky clothes he looked like the

Pillsbury Doughboy on maneuvers. Seized by a Jack London mood, he spit to see if his saliva would freeze before it hit the ground. It did not, but we all watched, expecting tiny pellets to bound away like hailstones.

Bill discovered during breakfast that he was not properly dressed for the weather, a discovery that surprised nobody but him. He has always relied too heavily on his native hardiness, a constitution that allows him to put in eight-hour days on a construction crew, then spend three or four hours at home feeding his various livestock, busting ice from the water trough, repairing fences, plowing the driveway with his tractor—all the while dressed only in jeans and a Carhart jacket and seldom bothering with a hat or gloves. He wore a hat now, a stocking cap perched on his head to cover the bald spot, but it did not cover his ears. He also wore a pair of jersey gloves, though they got wet while he cut dead saplings for the breakfast fire and he never got around to drying them out. His boots, the kind of buckle galoshes we hated so much when our mothers made us wear them over our school shoes, were pulled over leather work boots. He wore his work jacket and blue jeans (but not insulated underwear—his bare knee, red as a boiled lobster, poked through a split in the jeans). When we questioned the wisdom of his attire he silenced us with a look. The look said we're here to canoe, by God, so cut the nonsense and let's get on with it. The rest of us were layered in polypropylene, Gore-Tex, Thinsulate, goose down, and wool, wore waterproof, insulated gloves and boots, had wool hats and face masks rolled down to cover everything but our eyes and small oval mouths. We felt a little ashamed of ourselves. Everyone except Bill seemed to have softened with the years.

This morning the woods were deep with fresh, dry snow and the sky was so blue and still that snow crystals sifted down apparently from nowhere. The river flowed thick with slush, like an unflavored Slurpee, just one or two degrees from freezing solid. Somebody mentioned a trip years earlier on the Au Sable—I missed that one, alas—when the surface of the river froze solid after a night during which the temperature reached twenty below zero, and they were forced to push the canoes ahead of them over the ice. It took hours to travel the mile or two before they found water fast enough to resist freezing. Now nobody could remember if it was on that same trip that Scott Bulecki's sleeping bag caught fire. They spurned tents in those days, slept in the open or in carelessly dug snow caves, and while asleep Scott grew cold in his cheap sleeping bag and edged closer and closer to the fire until the fabric began to smolder. He woke in time to prevent himself from being burned, but not before the bag was destroyed. He spent the remainder of the night sitting on a log, tending the fire.

As we talked we loaded the canoes, careful to wrap our tents, sleeping bags, and extra clothes tightly in waterproof bags, sealing them inside duffels, Duluth Packs, and five-gallon plastic pails with waterproof lids, then strapping everything securely and evenly inside the canoes. Mike and Mark took the last crunching steps around the campsite to be sure we had forgotten nothing. Then we got on with it.

In our group only Bill advocates aluminum canoes. He likes them because they stand up to a lot of mistreatment and can be pounded back into shape with a mallet, something he likes to do. But the harsh metal wicks the heat from your lower body and draws it toward the river in nature's tireless effort toward equilibrium. We're immediately aware of that on the water, where it's obvious that we are the aberrations in a winter landscape: pathetic and inefficient furnaces struggling to keep warm in the midst of all this cold. We do not want our canoes sucking away any more warmth.

We paddled hard because the exertion warmed us and because it always feels good to be on the water in the morning. Craig mentioned, for perhaps the hundredth time in two days, that a cold day of canoeing is still better than a warm day of work. Bill broke a paddle. Mike, always prepared for emergencies, passed his spare—our only spare—to Bill. We paddled around a sweeping bend and surprised three white-tailed deer bedded down on the bank beside the river. They could not have looked more surprised if we had been a troupe of dancing bears in gypsy costumes. We drifted past, close enough to see the tiny plumes of breath around their snouts, then paddled hard again through a long, narrow corridor where snow-crested cedars leaned over the river, and the water, perfect mirror of the sky, seemed hardly altered by current.

Bill broke his second paddle.

Mark shrugged.

Just another day in the salt mines.

Too Many
Ontonagons

It was love at first sight, and in the least likely of places: a tavern in the tiny crossroads village of Nestoria, in the western Upper Peninsula. Nestoria is best known as the setting for a delightful Robert Traver story titled "Paulson, Paulson, Everywhere." Its secondary claim to fame comes from having a bar served by the loveliest, sweetest-tempered bartendress you'd ever hope to meet. Craig Date and I, river-bumming across the U.P., could not have been more surprised. She was tall, graceful, with a waterfall of thick black hair, dressed in a sleeveless T-shirt and a pair of dead-in-your-tracks jeans. While we watched, dazed, she leaned on the bar sipping diet soda and talked about her passion for exploring the local backcountry by canoe and Jeep. When we stammered in sympathy she signaled for quiet. The jukebox had just kicked in with "Your Cheating Heart," the original, sung by old Hank himself, and she wanted to hear it.

Craig fell furiously in love. Even I, who am married to a girl every bit as lovely, was smitten. But it hit Craig harder. It hit him so hard that early one morning a week later he insisted we drive to that same tavern for breakfast. It made no difference to him that Nestoria was nearly a hundred miles away, or that we had planned to travel in the opposite direction that day. We went, we had a fine breakfast, but it was the girl's day off. Craig, love-struck to boldness, asked where she might be. Trout fishing, we were told. On the Ontonagon.

I t's difficult to ignore the sheer number of Ontonagons that wind across the western Upper Peninsula of Michigan. At widely spaced bridges you cross a middle branch, a south branch, an east branch, a west branch, and a mainstream— each offering a glimpse of a river startlingly different from the last. The various branches range from slow to fast, from clear to murky, from clay red to chocolate brown. They're different enough to be like half-sisters, or like those siblings you sometimes see that appear to have sprung from separate genetic lines, one tow-headed, one freckled and red-haired, one an odd mix of gray eyes, brown hair, and pale complexion. Craig was determined to track down the goddess/bartendress. I wanted to investigate the mystery of the Ontonagons.

In the bar that morning, over bacon and eggs, I asked the room in general about fishing and canoeing on the local rivers. One of the locals recommended we put into the South Branch at Ewen and paddle downstream to Victoria Dam.

We pulled out topographical maps. "What about Flannigan Rapids?" we asked. "Any substance to them?"

"Nah, dem rapids is nuthin.' Dey don't even raise a good splash."

"Have you actually canoed that stretch yourself?" we asked. ,

"Well, no, I haven't. But my brudder-in-law, Oren, he canoed it once in 1968, I tink."

Twenty-five years ago. Not so long, really, in the grand scheme of things.

We found the river running high, flush to its banks. No clarity here: The water was the color of gourmet coffee, say mocha, with too much cream. We parked at the access site beside the bridge in Ewen and launched our canoe.

Some confusion arises because the South Branch, not many miles below Ewen, joins with the West Branch and adopts that river's name, in spite of the West Branch being a smaller stream made desperately dry most of the year by a dam at Lake Gogebic. When the water's high in spring the West Branch contains some whitewater in a wooded valley flanked by bluffs once mined for copper. But the water goes down quickly. By late spring it's little more than a creek, filtering into the South Branch over a spillage of rocks and gravel. Friends and I once spent a day dragging our canoes and kayaks over six miles of its dry bed.

The South Branch—and the West Branch after the two

join together—was well mannered and relaxing most of its length. But late in the day, just before the river ended at Victoria Pond, we came around a bend and heard a locomotivelike roar and saw mist rising above nasty waves.

We paddled to shore and got out to take a look. The river dropped over a rock shelf and rose up below it in a wave standing five feet high. Beyond it was a succession of diminishing waves, each pounding angrily in a different direction, chopped up by rocks and other ledges. A midstream channel seemed runnable, but waves loomed up on both sides and looked ready to pounce. It would be like canoeing through a gap in the front line of a football team. We considered our options.

We were, to be honest, scared. Our canoe, a Sawyer Cruiser, is fine for moderate current but has low freeboard and doesn't turn quickly, which are poor qualities in whitewater. Also, as nearly as we could figure, we were fifteen miles from the nearest road and had not seen a human being all day. There was a chance that a mishap would result in more than bruised egos.

Still, that center channel looked runnable. We viewed it from upstream and down, from the river's edge and from a ledge above it. In time it began to look less imposing. We decided to run the sucker.

It wasn't as bad as we expected. It would have been easy except that we went up on a rock at the lip of the drop and turned sideways. We slipped over the ledge, hit the first wave, took on some water, and spun downstream barely avoiding the largest rock, a Volkswagen of a boulder awash in waves.

Ducking into calm water near shore we thrust our paddles skyward and bellowed at the river for not being man enough to unman us. At that moment we spotted, in the shallows beside us, the remains of a canoe that had been twisted like aluminum foil around a rock. It was like those classic Death Valley scenes, where a dehydrated traveler drinks deeply from a pool of water then raises his eyes to see a human skull grinning at him from the opposite bank.

Craig gazed at the twisted canoe, a wistful look in his eyes. "We could have died here," he said, "and she would never even know."

The East Branch we were familiar with by reputation. Friends had once, during their college days, followed the advice of an ill-informed forest service employee and launched their canoes in its upper reaches near the town of Kenton. They were using a pair of aluminum prototypes built from industrial-grade metal, with rivets the size of half-dollars, and a twenty-foot fiberglass-over-wood monstrosity they called "The Whitewater Special." It was owned by a party animal named Reggie who was intensely proud of it, though he admitted he had never paddled the thing, having acquired it in trade from somebody who owed him money over a failed drug deal. "The Whitewater Special" was no doubt an elegant and carefully crafted canoe, but it required three men to lift it down from the car racks. Also, it leaked, so nothing perishable could be placed in it. That meant the aluminum boats had to be loaded with more than their share of gear, causing them to ride lower than recommended in the water. But the boys would not be discouraged. They set off in good spirits, made two miles in no time at all down the tightly winding little river, and came up hard against the first logjam. It was the kind of logjam you might see in your nightmares. It rose fifteen feet above the river and was composed of enormous silver logs tumbled together like matchsticks in a kitchen blender. My friends portaged around the logjam by dragging the loaded boats with ropes, rather the way Egyptian laborers moved stones to the Pyramids. That first jam was only a few hundred yards long. Subsequent jams were longer and followed one another in relentless sequence, with only short sections of open water between. The grandfather of all logjams appeared the third day. Reports varied, but our friends claimed it was a mile long, rose eighty feet in the air, and was being disassembled, one log at a time, by a well-built and exceedingly tall fellow with a blue ox.

Craig and I chose to canoe the other end of the river, a seven-mile stretch of mostly continuous light rapids. It's a quick and rock-studded sprint to the junction with the mainstream, through a steep valley of hardwoods. Unfortunately the water is so discolored by suspended clay and silt that you can't see rocks even a few inches beneath the surface. We bounced off them most of the way.

By the time we neared the end of the river the sun was low, glaring off the water. I closed my eyes to rest them and noticed how diverse the sounds of the river were. In the foreground were murmuring, whispering, chuckling vocalizations; in the background, gurgles, gargles, and glubs. Now and then came a few ringings and a tinkle, even an occasional thud and dull whacking. The canoe slipping through the water made a sound like silk being torn.

We hit a rock dead on, stopping us, and I slid off my seat to the bottom of the canoe.

Craig turned around and looked at me in surprise. "What happened?" he asked.

"Hit a rock."

"Sorry," he said. "Didn't see it."

Looking around, he said, "This is the kind of place a lady would fish."

The Middle Branch is the classiest of the Ontonagon sisters, a clear-water trout stream rising out of a cluster of clean highland ponds in the Sylvania Recreation Area. We put into the river upstream of the town of Watersmeet on a cold, blustery afternoon, and I immediately began catching uncommon numbers of uncommonly large brook trout. The stream was crammed with them, all apparently starving. We tied up to a tree trunk above a deep run of fast water and I caught three twelve-inchers in three casts. I tossed my small Mepps spinner downstream and it was grabbed by a brook trout at least fifteen inches long, the largest I had ever hooked. As I reached for it with a landing net it tossed the spinner and escaped.

"Damn!" I cried. "Did you see that?"

"See what?" Craig asked.

The mainstream of the Ontonagon flows for fifteen miles from the junction of the East, Middle, and West branches to Lake Superior at the town of Ontonagon. On that broad expanse of river we encountered whitecaps raised by a furious Lake Superior wind funneling upstream along the valley. The wind blew much faster upstream than the current flowed downstream, creating an interesting conflict of forces. When we slowed our paddling for even a moment our forward progress stopped and we began drifting upstream. We covered the fifteen miles to Ontonagon in eight hours of continuous hard paddling. Craig volunteered to hitchhike back to the truck.

While I waited for him I rested on the bank and thought about the past few days. The Ontonagon was an interesting and unusual river system, and we'd had fun exploring it, but I was disappointed that all our time on the water hadn't satisfied some deeper needs in me. Craig, whom I've known since college, when we used to stay up all night talking passionately about such things, once told me that when he paddled a canoe for even a few hours he became so relaxed that his mind emptied of every thought and image and became as lucid as a fishbowl. I was envious. My own head was still filled with the usual snarls of mental chatter. On the other hand, I knew that canoeing (and fishing) could help a person learn—or relearn, since most of us were splendidly equipped for it as children—the gentle art of goofing off. Away in a canoe, removed from the gripping hands of society, we're free to be wholly, wonderfully unproductive. With no one watching, the urge returns to lie back and watch clouds.

I mentioned these things to Craig when he returned

with the truck, and asked him if he thought it was possible to achieve some sort of mystical union with nature by spending as much time in it as we did. If so, I asked, why was it that after four days' canoeing down delightful rivers in beautiful country I still couldn't get the theme song to "Gilligan's Island" out of my head? He didn't have an answer.

We loaded our equipment in the back of the truck and secured the canoe to the racks. It was my turn to drive.

Thirty miles down the road we crossed a bridge marked with a sign that read "Cisco Branch of the Ontonagon."

A sixth sister! We had not heard of this one, and I wondered out loud if we should pull over and consult the maps. Craig, looking at distant hills through the side window, apparently didn't hear me. I suggested the Ontonagon was guilty of excess, and said again that we should probably investigate on the chance that the Cisco Branch was the finest branch of all. He said nothing.

I'd seen him this way before. We had to get as far from Nestoria as possible. I turned on the radio, found the country station, and kept driving.

WARRING FACTIONS

It is September 24, Craig Date's birthday, and we have paddled the lengths of eight rivers in thirteen days. This is definitely not the way to spiritual enrichment. We are somewhere on a river in a remote portion of the Upper Peninsula, besieged by bitter wind and cold rain, and Craig and I have not spoken for three days. At first there was no malice involved; we simply ran out of things to say. We grew weary of each other the way married couples can grow weary after twenty-five years of too much work and too few vacations. That was at first. Now I'm not so sure. Now there seems to be plenty of malice involved.

As stern paddler I have looked far too long at Craig's back. It is an ordinary back with little to recommend it. I have learned to hate it. It is expressionless. It appears to be

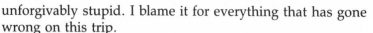
unforgivably stupid. I blame it for everything that has gone wrong on this trip.

I make an effort to be jolly, which prods Craig into silent anger, which of course is why I do it. When I suggest he paddle left around a midstream rock, he pretends not to hear and paddles right, which enrages me, which is of course why he does it. We have stomped out the perimeters of our friendship.

It is late in the day, the gray sky turning charcoal, and we cannot find a place to camp. Two likely spots are rejected by Craig for various (unclear) reasons, and when he points out a site he considers acceptable I veto it (too brushy, too hilly) on principle. So we are even. Except now it's nearly dark and the easy rain that has been falling since mid-afternoon has turned to sleet that rattles against the canoe and stings our faces. We are equipped with a good tent and warm sleeping bags, but they will do us little good if we can't find a place to spread them.

We've entered a region of marshes where waving cattails and bulrushes disappear to the horizon in every direction. The river has widened and slackened; channels splinter away into the marsh. Craig can't resist: "Should have taken that

last campsite like I wanted to," he says without turning. "What are we supposed to do now, spend the night in a goddamned swamp?"

I make grotesque faces at his back.

It is dark when we stop finally, pulling the canoe onto a tiny hummock of land sprouting a thicket of spruce and birch. We explore it by flashlight. There is no level ground. We hack out enough space to pitch the tent, positioning it so our feet at least will point downhill. By morning we'll be crumpled to the bottom of the tent, like pizzas tipped in their delivery box. We attempt briefly to build a fire, but there is nothing dry to burn on the island and we don't have the patience to work at it. We eat a quick meal of cold soup and go to bed.

My sleeping bag is damp and cold. Roots jab my back. For the thirteenth night in succession I accuse myself of stupidity for failing to pack a sleeping pad and a pillow. I find myself fantasizing about restaurant meals and motel rooms with unlimited hot water and cable TV.

Then, somehow, not because I want to, I remember this is Craig's birthday. He's thirty-one years old, far from home and loved ones. I have not, of course, bought a gift.

"Hey," I say into the darkness. "Happy birthday."

There is silence. I suspect he's analyzing my words for hidden meaning.

"Shut up," he says.

"Thanks," he says.

CANOEING
MICHIGAN'S
WILDEST RIVER

In the summer of 1985 Craig Date and I decided to canoe the Presque Isle, Michigan's most challenging whitewater river. For months we'd been paddling rivers all over the state, and everywhere we went we heard people talking in hushed and reverent tones about the Presque Isle. We were cocky enough to doubt what we heard.

We learned, however, that the Presque Isle is not the kind of river you can take lightly. That point was brought to our attention at Piers Gorge on the Menominee River, many miles from the Presque Isle. Piers Gorge is itself one of the best-known stretches of whitewater in the Midwest, a half-mile cataract where the generally sedate, three-hundred-foot-wide Menominee gets forced through an eighty-foot-wide canyon. The day we visited the gorge about twenty kayakers were taking turns running through what, in their own lexicon, are known as haystacks, rollers, souse holes, surfers, and stoppers. Their lithe boats, colorful as carnival flags, danced over chutes and falls, through waves, into and quickly out of frothing holes. One boat banked into an eddy beneath the rock ledge where we stood.

Shouting to be heard above the river, we asked the kayaker if he knew anything about the Presque Isle River in the western corner of the Upper Peninsula. He had heard of it, he said, and knew someone who had paddled it. He pointed to a gold-colored kayak across the river, and before we could say more, darted away to the far shore, dodging waves and holes. In a moment the gold kayak rested beside us. In it was a young woman. Yes, she had heard of the river. No, she had never paddled it. But she knew someone who had. She peeled out of the eddy with one of the dramatic downstream leans kayakers practice endlessly.

Another kayak met us at the eddy, a pure-white one paddled by a calm young man. Yes, he had heard of the river. Yes, he had paddled it. Twice. What did we want to know?

That year Craig and I were doing research for a paddling guide to the rivers of Michigan, and had put together a tentative list of rivers we wanted to explore. Three rivers in the western Upper Peninsula—the Montreal, Black, and Presque Isle—drew our attention because we had heard they contained the most challenging rapids in the state. Two of them, the Montreal and the Black, were said to be fast, interesting rivers that deserved to be in a book about the state's best canoeing rivers. But the third, the Presque Isle, presented some problems. All we knew for certain about it was that it was interrupted by numerous waterfalls, that it flowed north along the edge of the Porcupine Mountains Wilderness State Park, and that it emptied into Lake Superior. Any other information was sketchy and ambiguous. One publication listed it as a navigable river, but for "experts only," and that it should be attempted only by whitewater fanatics. Another described it as "a wild, magnificent river in rugged country," and added that there were "too many portages to be enjoyable." An outdated reference book applauded the river as offering "the wildest trip in the state because this stream is fast, flowing through rugged country, but it is a magnificent river and therefore worth the effort." Fine praise, but the book went on to describe the river flowing a hundred miles in the wrong direction, into Lake Michigan.

We learned a little from other canoeists. One said the river was simply unrunnable. Another said it could be floated in rafts but not canoes. A veteran paddler who had made many trips down well-known Wisconsin rivers had never paddled the Presque Isle but had heard enough about it to lend us something of a perspective: "Are you kidding? You're talking about Class 6 rapids. That river's at the bottom of my list. I'm saving it in case I ever go insane."

Class 6 rapids, if you're unfamiliar with the American Whitewater Association's system for rating whitewater, is definitely a category best suited to lunatics. Designed as a standard to judge river difficulty, the system designates rapids in classes ranging from 1 for the simplest, to 6 for the most difficult to negotiate. Typical rapids in the kinds of rivers favored by families or beginning paddlers rate a solid Class 1: "Moving water with a few riffles and small waves; few or no obstructions." Some stretches, especially in the spring when water is high, might rate Class 2: "Easy rapids with waves up to three feet and wide, clear channels that are obvious without scouting; some maneuvering is required." Class 3 is described as having "high, irregular waves often capable of swamping an open canoe; narrow passages that require complex maneuvering." Class 4: "Require precise maneuvering in very turbulent waters; conditions make rescue difficult; generally not possible for open canoes." Class 5: "Extremely difficult, long and very violent; significant hazard to life." And Class 6: "Difficulties of Class 5 carried to the extreme of navigability; nearly impossible and very dangerous."

About the time we decided it would be best to quietly ignore the Presque Isle we came across an article in *Canoe* magazine that listed it as one of ten North American rivers that "define the outer edge of contemporary whitewater paddling." The article quoted a whitewater paddler named Fred Young, who claimed the river was the best whitewater run in the Midwest. Months later in a bar in Ironwood we would see a photograph of Fred Young, or "Fearless Fred" as he was known locally. The photo showed him going over the edge of a thirty-foot waterfall in a decked canoe. His head was tipped back and his mouth gaped open. It was difficult to tell if he was expressing terror or pleasure. It looked, in truth, like he was singing.

We spent the winter preparing for an expedition down the Presque Isle. We studied topographic maps and whitewater manuals, and collected much of the equipment we would need, including a pair of Royalex whitewater canoes. The greatest problem facing us was our own doubt about our abilities as whitewater paddlers. We had learned to canoe on the free-flowing but civilized rivers of the northern Lower Peninsula, and our only whitewater experience was limited to those rivers' light rapids and riffles. If the Presque Isle was as awesome as evidence suggested, we would definitely be outclassed by it.

Humility brought us to Piers Gorge on the Menominee River. We were looking for help and hoped this kayaker with experience on the Presque Isle could give us some. "Tough river," he said. "Maybe the toughest east of the Rockies." He explained that the problem was a relatively narrow range of runnable water levels. If the water was too low, rocks made passage impossible; too high and it was simply too dangerous. He ran it twice, he said, on consecutive weekends. The first time he and his party made it through without serious mishap. The following weekend the water level was up six inches due to rain and they were forced to portage many stretches of the most furious rapids. One of their group capsized, lost his boat, and was forced to walk out through ten miles of forest—the final three hours of it in the dark.

Meanwhile the woman in the gold kayak had returned. She said she knew of one group of six kayakers, all highly advanced paddlers, who went down the Presque Isle. Only one came out with his boat.

I told them we were thinking of running the river in open canoes. The woman peeled out downstream as if to avoid the thought. The man stayed. He seemed polite, intelligent, and thoughtful, not someone to blurt out whatever came to his mind. But I could see it in his eyes. He thought we were crazy. We had just watched him ride rodeo-style through waves and holes powerful enough to swallow cabin cruisers, and he thought we were reckless lunatics.

"I doubt if you could make it," he said.

Our first glimpse of the Presque Isle came as something of a surprise. It was from the bridge at Highway M-28, south of the Porcupine Mountains, east of the town of Wakefield in the Upper Peninsula's Gogebic County. Four of us stood on the bridge—Craig and I, plus old friends Mark Wilkes and Mike McCumby—double-checking maps to be sure we had the right river. Instead of churning whitewater we found a river as slow, discolored, and unexciting as any we had ever seen. Drowned trees were piled at the bridge abutments; vines hung from muddy banks; water striders skated leisurely across the river. You could tell upstream from down only by the blades of aquatic grasses lying pointed to the north.

It was difficult to believe that a few miles downstream this quiet and peaceful river goes crazy. We knew from our research that it descends eighteen miles through a flurry of falls and rapids until it meets Lake Superior. In the first 9 miles it would drop an average of 17.5 feet for every mile of length, enough descent to create some interesting rapids, especially if that descent was compressed into a few sections of the river instead of being spread out over the entire length. In the final 9 miles, commencing at a remote logging bridge known as Steiger's Bridge, the Presque Isle drops toward Lake Superior an average of 46.5 feet per mile. At the heart of that section is the Gorge, a solid mile of rapids and falls where the river drops 140 feet, and the banks, we imagined, were littered with the bones of foolhardy canoeists and kayakers.

We launched our canoes at the M-28 bridge about noon one day in early June. Already we had spent a week warming up on Class 3 rapids on the Montreal and Black, fine whitewater rivers in their own right, and were feeling confident. We felt we had mastered those rivers. How bad could the Presque Isle be?

There is a misleading allure to the first few miles of the

Presque Isle. Pools the size of small lakes are connected by minor chutes and rapids that barely need attention. We drifted through them while eating sandwiches.

Gradually the rapids begin coming a bit more frequently and with a bit more intensity. The changes, at first, are almost too subtle to notice. We negotiated a number of the short, abrupt ledge drops we came to recognize as characteristic of much of the river. They began to come in series, and to increase in size.

It's difficult to say whether Minnewawa Falls is the name of a particular falls, or if it is the collective name of all the falls, chutes, drops, and ledges we found spread out over that quarter-mile length of river. It may be impossible to separate one component from the other, though each has distinct and frightening characteristics. We always knew what was coming by the roaring audible from around the next bend, or by the way the river suddenly disappeared in a horizon drop. The difficult thing about a horizon drop is that it is often impossible to tell how high the drop is or where the best place to run it is until the nose of your canoe is practically to the edge of it. The only sensible thing to do in such instances is go to shore and investigate, deciding then whether the water should be run or portaged.

In that regard we managed the first portions of Minnewawa well. The initial sets of drops were tricky but not all that difficult. We came down through a couple of two-foot drops into a three-footer, then past a jumble of boulders where the river has been compressed to about thirty feet wide, then down a pair of drops into a still pond. We alternated running it and taking photographs. It was fun.

The second leg, and maybe this was the real Minnewawa, was a little trickier. It comes after a short stretch of intense, boulder-studded rapids and begins with a three-foot-high ledge that crosses the entire river. Most of the water is funneled to the left, where it dumps into a frothing pool barely large enough for a pivoting canoe. From there it turns ninety degrees to the right around a rock the size of a small house, then ninety degrees to the left through a twenty-foot-wide chasm. The river is forced through the chasm with the kind of velocity you achieve by pressing your thumb over the end of a garden hose. Immediately below the chasm the river dumps into one of those lake-sized ponds.

Mark and I, in the first canoe, made it through in fine shape, taking in just a few inches of water at the final chute between the rocks. We set up position below the rapids, ready with cameras and a throw rope.

When the second canoe came into view it was apparent something was wrong. The angle of approach wasn't right and in the tight confines of the rapids Craig and Mike weren't able to correct it before they hit the chute of water in the chasm. By the time they entered it they were already swamped. The first big wave capsized them.

Afterward they described the sensation of swimming in water that was more air than H_2O. They talked about how it refused to float them, even in their bulky flotation vests, how it was yellow, swirling, and furious, how it seemed to suck the air from their lungs. They described the way it felt to be plunged underwater and tumbled downstream knowing that a submerged canoe carrying more than a ton of water was following behind them waiting for a rock to put them in the middle of the classic immovable object/unstoppable force dilemma. They came up sputtering in the big pool. The canoe, slightly battered and stripped of the flotation bags we had harnessed inside, rolled and wallowed on the surface.

The remainder of the way to Steiger's Bridge we worked to overcome a sudden attack of uncertainty. Every rapids—and there were more and more of them—took on new significance. Serious accident and injury now seemed a real possibility. We portaged the second major drop in the upper stretch, a fifteen-foot-high waterfall named Nimikon Falls. We learned later that Nimikon is sometimes run by kayakers warming up for the heavy water below Steiger's Bridge. It was apparent to us that if we were going to complete the trip beyond that bridge we would need some help.

The next day we talked to a number of local paddlers. All agreed that we had paddled the easy half of the river, but when we asked if they would lead us through the difficult half they were all suddenly busy.

We finally reached a whitewater guide named Wayne Overberg who lived in Eagle River, Wisconsin, seventy-five miles south of the Presque Isle. He told us over the phone that he had run the river just a few weeks earlier and it was still very fresh in his mind. That was the good news. The bad news was he had broken his ankle in the effort and was in a plaster cast. Not that it would slow him down.

Overberg met us at our campground in the morning. He was a cheerful thirty-year-old man, bearded and robust. During the drive to the river he told us what to expect. The water was extremely intense. There were at least six miles of continuous Class 2, 3, and 4 rapids. A few drops that reached Class 5 would have to be portaged. The rapids started immediately below Steiger's Bridge and got progressively worse until you entered the Gorge, and then they got worse yet. He had broken his ankle from the impact of striking a rock with the nose of his kayak. Of the five paddlers in his party, two had broken their ankles and only one had actually completed the trip.

At the river Overberg was struck by how much the water level had dropped since he was last there. It appeared to have fallen two or three feet, which meant many of the drops considered Class 4 or 5 would be probably no worse than Class 3 or 4. He began wrapping his cast in plastic bags and sealing it with duct tape. "This is going to be a gravy run," he said.

A light drizzle fell as we unloaded the boats from our cars and ran a check on paddles, cameras, watertight bags of dry clothes, first-aid kits, matches, and lunches. We wedged spare paddles into firm but easily reached nooks. We tightened our flotation vests and cinched down our helmets. We left our wallets with our wives.

The current was strong, commanding, and white-capped even in the relatively tame water near the bridge. A cold wind came upstream, pushing banks of fog from Lake Superior into our faces. It began to rain.

Overberg saw we needed to be distracted so he encouraged us to practice our draw strokes, pry strokes, and eddy turns. Within a few minutes he had us ducking and sashaying into eddies behind rocks, drawing and bracing on our paddles, as eager to please as schoolchildren. We made our way downstream, the cold and rain forgotten.

The water grew progressively wilder. Wayne disappeared over a drop below us, the stern of his kayak flagging in the air as he went over, and we could see him only from the neck up as he waited below. He motioned toward the center of the river, away from the chute he had just run, where it was obvious the major flow of the current was funneled.

Mark and I paddled laterally across the river through fast, shallow water, but we kept striking rocks that acted like pinball bumpers to force us toward the heavy current at the inside channel. By now we were close enough to see a furious drop full of large, conflicting waves, and we wanted no part of it. Unexpectedly, we bumped a rock and were spun around backward in the current. For a moment, at the brink of the drop, we entered a slick of calm water, and by using draw strokes on opposite sides of the canoe managed to pivot most of the way around just as we went over the edge. The waves hit us, and a sidecurler—a nasty variety of wave formed by the opposition of two tongues of current—dumped half a boatload of water into the canoe. We wallowed through the waves somehow and made it to a tiny sandbar.

For the next six miles of nonstop rapids the only opportunity to rest was behind rocks, in eddies not much larger than our canoes themselves. We were relieved to discover that the Class 6 drops we had heard about had indeed been reduced to a mere Class 4. But they still looked deadly to us.

"Want to run it?" Wayne would ask, eyes bright, while

we were already lifting the canoes up rocky bluffs to go around a fierce drop. One fifteen-foot drop caused the river to shoot up and over it like a giant pompadour, curls spilling down both sides. "What would that do to a canoe?" I asked. Overberg didn't hesitate. "Eat it," he said.

The Gorge, that infamous mile-long section where the river drops 140 feet, is a steep valley with wooded sides 120 to 150 feet high. The river descends a long protracted waterfall there. It begins with a trio of ledges known as Triple Drop. Wipe out in Triple Drop and your pieces don't start showing up for at least a mile.

We dragged the boats up the bluffs and Overberg led us inland to logging trails. We portaged our canoes and equipment along the trails to the end of the Gorge and lowered the boats down a steep bank to the river. Nakomis Falls, the climax of the Gorge, made an imposing sight upstream. Even below it the water was wild.

Overberg's eyes got a look we had seen in the eyes of the kayakers at Piers Gorge. He said we were now unhindered by major falls—except Lepisto, where he had broken his ankle, and Iagoo, which he had never seen because he'd been carried out through the woods. He began leading us through water we would have portaged upstream.

By now we operated on instinct, our attention narrowed to fine focus: find the best route, draw, pry, brace. Details like terrain and weather failed to register. Somewhere along the way the rain stopped. We portaged Lepisto Falls, all of us, and Overberg nosed his kayak upstream to the ledge that had broken his ankle.

Below Lepisto the drops and rapids began to diminish in intensity and we realized we had entered the protected forest of Porcupine Mountains Wilderness State Park. For the first time we noticed virgin pines and hemlocks towering over the forest. An eagle's nest the size of a picnic table dominated a massive red pine. White-tipped waves splashed casually. The sun came out. We went around a bend and there was the bridge at South Boundary Road with our wives and children lined up waving.

Somewhere upstream, in the last stretch below the portage at Lepisto Falls, we had undergone a transformation. Call it a graduation. Overberg said we had become solid intermediate whitewater paddlers. Not experts, but not duffers either, by God.

We had paddled right over Iagoo Falls. At least we think we did. They're marked clearly on maps, but perhaps they're only a minor falls that don't stand out from the other drops along the way. Or maybe we just ran them. Maybe we had our heads back and were singing.

JUST ME AND
MY JACKET

My wife can't understand why I choose to remain ignorant of outdoor fashions. Contrary to what she thinks, I do not hate clean clothes or hope secretly for opportunities to roll around in mud. I admit I prefer well-worn clothing, but I don't necessarily want it unwashed. It's true that as a child I slept with my dog, but not until he had dried off from the day's explorations and never if he had rooted around that day in the fish that sometimes washed up dead on the beach near our house. I might be a bit of a slob, but I have certain standards.

The truth is, when it comes to clothing, I just can't keep up with technology. While many of my friends have been converted to Gore-Tex and Thermax and those other super-synthetics that were discovered accidentally in corporate

laboratories and tested in outer space, my favorite article of
clothing remains a red-and-black wool hunting jacket. It is a
jacket essentially unchanged since the days of ax-slinging
lumberjacks. My grandfather wore one just like it, along with
red wool pants that fastened snugly around his ankles. Seeing
me in my jacket, Gail once suggested that in a previous life I
inhabited an unchinked log cabin near James Bay and passed
my days on snowshoes, tending a trap-line, and making
smoked jerky out of hunks of moose meat. It's an attractive
idea.

Any jacket as dependable, warm, and comforting as
mine is worth defending to the death. Unlike the modern
synthetic models I've handled, mine is pleasantly heavy. You
know you're wearing it. It's as satisfying to heft around on
your shoulders as a well-loaded backpack. It's durable in the
manner of good leather boots and it's equipped with so many
pockets I'm still discovering new ones. Pockets are important
to me. I like to put my hands inside and be surprised at what
I find: a flattened pack of Doublemint, a book of impotent
matches, pinecones, fossils, a berserk compass, one jersey
glove, a magnifying glass, a twenty-gauge shotgun shell, a
grouse feather, a packet of crumpled and arcane notes to
myself. Whenever any small but important object comes up
missing around home my kids automatically look in Dad's
jacket pockets. Even if it's not there they come away con-
tented, certain to have discovered something of equal or
greater value.

These days, when so many people outdoors appear to
have stepped from the pages of an L. L. Bean catalog and
invariably examine the labels on your clothing before they
meet your eyes, it's satisfying to believe fashion is irrelevant.
I want functional clothing that leaps beyond trends to comfort
and durability. My coat is appropriate whether I'm canoeing
on brisk September mornings or fishing for December
steelhead; it works equally well for grouse hunting, cross-
country skiing, hiking, or cutting firewood. When camping I
roll it inside a cotton sweatshirt and it becomes a pillow. In a
pinch I could use it to smother a brushfire or signal a rescue

plane. I can wad it, beat it, wipe my hands on it, drag it through brambles, toss it in a corner, stand on it barefoot while drying my socks over a fire, even spill Craig Date's industrial-formula Texas chili on it without fear of spontaneous combustion. If I were desperate enough I suspect I could boil it down into a nutritious broth. It never berates me for the abuse it suffers and it stays warm even when wet. And when wet it smells—faintly, just enough to recall old friends—like a wet golden retriever.

I realize my jacket needs washing, and has for several years, but the label under the collar says it must be dry-cleaned and I don't trust the chemical processes used in dry cleaning. Besides, you can't actually notice it needs washing unless you get very close. The red-and-black color scheme is designed to mask stains, and when dirty the wool improves in wearability and maybe even increases in insulation value.

My jacket and I will probably never be asked to model for the cover of *Gentleman's Quarterly*, but we can live with that. I figure it's the fashion world's loss.

THE HEEBIE-JEEBIES

*I believe that men are generally still a little
afraid of the dark . . .*

HENRY DAVID THOREAU, *WALDEN*

I for one am. A little. It's rather embarrassing and I probably wouldn't admit it except that I have taken an informal poll of those men and women I know who go outside alone at night to fish or camp or perform wildlife research, and all of them admit to a little uneasiness. It does not keep us from enjoying those nighttime pursuits, mind you. Let's just say we're jumpy; let's say our attention is sharpened to incredible alertness.

I know that in theory there is little to fear at night, especially in North America where we enjoy a position high up on the food chain. Except for the minor risk of venomous snakes, avalanches, tidal waves, tornadoes, falling trees, flooding rivers, lightning strikes, quicksand, deer ticks, rabid skunks, killer bees, scorpions, and black-widow spiders, we have every reason to stride with confidence through the valleys and mountains of our continent.

But theories become notoriously useless when you're standing waist-deep in a slow river, alone, midway through a night so dark you can see nothing but the faintest black outline of the trees against the sky, and some sudden, unexplained creature of startling size explodes in the water five feet from you. It's true, it's true: fear has a flavor, like Indianhead pennies. And another thing: you can hear your own heart pounding. It sounds like kids drumming on trash cans.

Anthropologists long ago proposed that night fears may have deep primordial sources passed down genetically from those ages when humans were fair game and had every reason to be afraid at night. Similarly, the innate fear of falling exhibited by newborn children might be explained as a genetic reminiscence of a time when our ancestors lived in trees.

That all seems logical enough, though it is of little comfort in the darkness. I tend to blame personal experience rather than evolution for my own uneasiness. Years ago, when Bud Haywood was introducing me to the joys of fishing at night for trout, he left me one evening on a sandbar in a section of the Boardman so sluggish and dark-spirited I had always been afraid to visit it even in daylight. With a warning not to step into the apparently bottomless pool before me, he crashed through the tag alders and disappeared somewhere upstream.

I waited through the dim light of dusk, until full darkness dropped over the world. It was the starless, humid, thick darkness of early July. At night, I learned, rivers can seem treacherous and malign, stirring up the imagination the way a booted foot swirls up silt. I tried a few casts into the pool but I was tentative, not really sure I wanted to be hooked to anything that lived there. Finally I just stood motionless in the river trying to imagine myself part of, rather than alien to, the darkness.

An object floated toward me on the water. It was visible only in the periphery of my vision, something so dark it was like a hole in the blackness, drifting downstream with the current until it was directly in front of me, less than a rod's length away. A clump of underbrush, I decided, or a half-submerged stump. I raised my rod to cast, and at that moment all of heaven and hell exploded in crashes of thunder and lightning and burning cinder and I shouted with the unrestrained abandon of the gloriously terrified. The object I had seen floating toward me—it took some time to realize this—had been a beaver clenching an aspen branch; my sudden movement had caused it to cannonball the water with its tail and dive for safety.

Bud laughed when I told him later what had happened. "That big old sonofabitch has been scarin' the bejesus out of fishermen as long as I can remember," he said. "It's best to just ignore him."

I was never the same after that. I continued to fish at night, but any movement, any unaccountable sound had me wincing like a gun-shy dog anticipating the shot.

Once you come down with a case of night fears, frightening events follow you mercilessly. I remember lying awake one night in 1975 in a small tent in the Yellowstone backcountry. Mike McCumby and I had hiked there in the morning and spent the day climbing after bighorn sheep on a mountainside, examining the scat of elk and coyote and bear, setting up camp finally beside a pond full of grayling and rainbow trout. Now Mike slept the good sleep of the innocent while I, excited by the day's explorations, lay warm and comfortable in my sleeping bag, listening to the breeze in the lodgepole pines and thinking about things. After a while I stopped thinking about things and started thinking about grizzly bears, which is a natural thing to do in a tent in the remote corners of Yellowstone. Those corners are, of course, grizzly country, a fact that until then had bothered me very little. The history of backcountry camping in Yellowstone is a long and bright one, and I knew there was very little chance of encountering a bear. But knowing it and believing it are very different things, and the more I thought it over the jumpier I became. Mike's easy, instant sleep had been amusing at first; now it seemed a betrayal. If he was any kind of friend, I reasoned, he would be awake to keep me company.

Then I heard a noise.

I have spent enough nights alone in a tent to know how imagination can amplify ordinary sounds. If you are sufficiently spooked a pair of raccoons fumbling with a cooler latch can sound like a Wyoming bar fight. Still, this seemed a significant noise, a notable noise. I considered it as objectively as possible. It was not a loud sound, not a definitive sound, just something out of audible place. On consideration, it seemed precisely the kind of furtive noise a very large creature would make if it did not want to be heard.

Now there came a large noise. Not a loud noise, a *large* noise, the sound of something very large stepping quietly on padded feet. Then definitely (oh, definitely) the sound of air being inhaled through spacious nostrils.

Dryness clenched my throat. It was impossible to swallow. Inside my chest, my heart galloped like a rodent trapped in an empty five-gallon bucket. Every cell of my body stood erect, listening. My eyes strained in vain to see something, anything, in the blackness inside the tent. I waited for a single exquisite claw to rent the fabric and open the wall of the tent, like a surgeon's scalpel slicing the cellophane that encloses a Hostess cupcake. I visualized the event so clearly I was unsure whether it had happened yet.

Two shambling revolutions around the tent and now a snuffling noise, as of sinus trouble.

Because I knew Mike would not want to die in the terrible oblivion of sleep, I tried to wake him. I whispered his name. The sound came out with so little volume it was not really a sound at all. Mike might have thought, were he awake, that he heard a field mouse yawning. He might have thought he heard the whispery voice of an ancestor buried six generations in his family's past. I tried again. The sound produced was less vocalization than telepathy, the message originating in my solar plexus but not pushed out by breath. I had no breath. My lungs hung void of air, like becalmed sails, the space inside my chest occupied only by the frantic leaping chaos of that trapped rodent.

Slowly, cautiously, I raised my arm from inside my sleeping bag and reached for Mike. I punched him. I punched him again, harder.

"What? What is it?" he said, his voice terribly, unbearably loud.

"Quiet. Bear. I think. Outside."

Mike probed in the darkness for his backpack, found a flashlight, and climbed from his sleeping bag. He unzipped the tent and poked his head out. He switched on the light. There was a pause, a very long pause. He came back inside and zipped the tent closed again.

"Porcupine," he said.

There was nothing, of course, I could say. I tried to chuckle but failed. For a moment I wondered if it would have been better had there been a bear. A grizzly. Snarling when Mike blinded it with the flashlight.

Mike settled back into his sleeping bag and switched the light off. The darkness seemed more complete, if that were possible. I thought about the nature of fear, how you can never remember afterward quite how it was. It's like trying to remember a smell: The gulf between the memory and the reality is too great to cross. Already I was beginning to forget just how frightened I had been.

"Yep, a porcupine," Mike said quietly. "Big one, though."

STURGEON, ON THE ICE, IN A FESTIVE MOOD

Small communities in the northern United States often find winter a dreary and profitless season, so they of course invent festivals to celebrate it. I prefer a raging case of cabin fever to the usual dull Winterfest, but I can sometimes be tempted by novelty. In the village of Onaway, in the northeast corner of Michigan's Lower Peninsula, an annual festival called the Black Lake Shivaree is designed to honor not its own dire self, but the sport of fishing for a magnificent fish that is only rarely caught: the lake sturgeon.

From an angler's point of view the most remarkable thing about lake sturgeon—other than the facts that they weigh from sixty to two hundred pounds, live to elephantine age, and are certainly among the world's ugliest fish—is that they are immune to conventional angling methods. They feed by sucking bottom mud through a vacuumlike snout that strains out food organisms, and if they ingest a fisherman's worm or minnow it is purely by accident. Anglers in quest of sturgeon have found it much more productive to utilize that most primitive of angling implements, the spear. They sit waiting in ambush in darkened, heated shacks on the ice hoping the five- and six-foot-long creatures will pass beneath them, an event that almost never occurs, so they can throw a heavy, multitined spear that almost always misses.

This is a carefully monitored practice. Although Michigan Department of Natural Resources biologists are convinced sturgeon are abundant enough in Black Lake and its sister lakes, Burt and Mullett, to withstand a great amount of spearing pressure, they have established stringent rules of the game. Any angler with a standard Michigan fishing license can try for sturgeon, but the spearing season lasts only for the month of February, no fish under fifty inches long may be speared, and only two sturgeon can be taken per angler per year. Almost no one limits out.

Some years Black Lake anglers are woefully unsuccessful. Only four fish were taken, for example, in 1988. Even in phenomenally good years only twenty or twenty-five will be speared. The weekend I visited the Shivaree, none of the three hundred or so attendees of the festival would have seen a sturgeon at all if a young man named David McCay hadn't driven home and returned with the sixty-two-pounder his father had speared earlier in the week and preserved frozen in a snowbank. It looked like something that died during the Pleistocene epoch and was recently hacked from a Siberian ice field.

One thing about small-town winter festivals: they're energetic. While I stood on the ice of Black Lake talking sturgeon spearing with David McCay, a raucous crowd in the circus tent nearby drank beer from Styrofoam cups and ate barbecued chicken to the accompaniment of live polka music. On a plowed racecourse on the ice, four-wheel all-terrain vehicles careened around the corners, their drivers wearing crash hel-

mets and masks that covered every inch of their skin. Some
hardy show-off with a hang glider allowed himself to be
towed on skis behind a snowmobile until he achieved suffi-
cient speed to lift off the ice, then caught the wind and circled
to an eerie height. It was cold enough to make your extremities ache, but smiling people wearing festival badges—each
depicting a sturgeon about to be poked in the back by a
spear—walked around without hats or gloves, cradling cups
of hot coffee in their hands.

Nobody within easy walking distance was fishing, but
a half-mile down the shoreline sat clusters of ice shanties with
plumes of smoke rising from their chimneys. Inside those
shanties sat men and women blessed with incredible reserves
of patience. David McCay's father, for instance, had already
spent every daylight hour of the past three weeks in his
shanty. The year before he had done the same and was re-
warded on the twenty-fifth of the month with a ninety-four-
pounder. "It pays to stick with it," he says. "The fish are
worth waiting for."

Sturgeon were not always so revered in this part of the
country. Early in the twentieth century dams were built
across the rivers that connect Black, Burt, and Mullett lakes

to Lake Huron, in the process landlocking sturgeon that had ascended to the lakes to spawn in their headwaters. In those days sturgeon were considered a rather magnificent trash fish, and were routinely speared from their shallow spawning streams and heaved on the banks or, at best, dragged to gardens and buried as fertilizer. It was not until society lights back east acquired a taste for caviar that anyone in Michigan considered the sturgeon useful. As soon as that happened the fish were in serious trouble. So many females were captured and stripped of their roe that the population was very nearly eliminated altogether.

Today, while still considered an oddity in many waters, lake sturgeon are not endangered. They inhabit all the Great Lakes and many connecting waters and are found in large lakes and rivers from Alberta, Canada, south to Nebraska and Missouri, and as far east as Labrador. And while Michigan's Black, Mullett, and Burt lakes are not the only places in North America where ice fishermen can spear sturgeon for sport, it is hard to imagine a place where they are pursued with more enthusiasm.

"This is the sturgeon headquarters of the whole area," Boyd Crist says, stepping into the bar of the Black Lake Hotel. Crist, a small, good-humored man of seventy who seems acquainted with everybody in sparsely populated Cheboygan County, is considered the guru of Black Lake sturgeon spearing. Since 1948, when he and his wife Doris opened a tackle shop and motel on the lake, he has killed about seventy-five sturgeon, making him what many consider the area's most successful sturgeon angler.

Sturgeon dominate the bar. Tacked along much of the length of one wall are several decades' worth of curled and yellowing snapshots of immense fish and beaming fishermen. Handwritten charts list the names of anglers next to the length and weight of their fish and the date they were caught. According the list, one recent year when twenty-five sturgeon were recorded, an incredible sixteen were taken the first day of the season (a record tainted by the rumor that a number of those fish were speared a few days earlier than the lawful opening of the season and had been harnessed beneath the ice until they could be legally brought into view). Several anglers claimed their two-fish season limit that first busy day.

Boyd Crist has known a few of those two-fish days himself, the equivalent of a hockey hat trick or a baseball pitcher's no-hitter. The accomplishment is all the more surprising when you consider that many Black Lake anglers pass the entire season without even seeing a sturgeon, and that it is not unusual for determined fishermen to go years on end without spearing one.

As a sideline to his tackle shop business, Crist rents ice shanties on Black Lake, stationing them over known hot spots and equipping them with heaters, spears, and other necessary equipment. The week before the Shivaree, customers in his fourteen shanties saw several fish, an encouraging spate of sightings, though none of the anglers hit the mark with their spears. Crist's shanties come stocked with large, heavily weighted wooden decoys shaped like red-and-white suckers, which are suspended near bottom to attract sturgeon. The decoys do not trigger predatory intent, only curiosity, giving the angler a badly needed edge. Still, the odds are in favor of the fish. In spite of the allure of the decoys, sturgeon often enter and leave spearing range quickly, or skirt the edges of it. Anglers are also prone to a variation of buck fever that causes spears to be thrown wild, Thermos bottles to be kicked into holes, and cords to be tangled around feet. The sight of a fish six-feet long and as wide across as a fair-sized alligator is enough to make some fishermen forget their spears altogether.

Although the experience of spearing and landing a sturgeon is said to be worth even years of waiting, the waiting is not necessarily the difficult part. One lifetime resident of the area recalls, as a boy, fishing for perch on the ice with hook and line and seeing a nearby shanty suddenly begin shaking. First one wall fell outward and crashed onto the ice, then another, then the third and fourth walls fell and the roof collapsed. A man was left standing in the open, hugging a gyrating six-foot sturgeon like a hideous dance partner, struggling to get it away from the hole and onto the ice.

Less severely damaged shanties are not uncommon. Sturgeon are extremely strong—capable, some anglers claim, of breaking a person's legs and arms in the tight confines of a spearing shanty. A solitary angler who has struck a fish will usually shout for assistance. In the few moments it takes to haul the fish hand-over-hand to the surface, a neighboring angler can be at his door. If the fish is not well speared—held by only one tine, say, or hit near the tail—the second fisherman will heave another spear into it. He can also help by being ready with a gaff. Everyone agrees most battles are lost when the fish is at the surface and must be lifted from the water. A gaff hooked in the jaw allows the fish to be dragged from the water head first, then hauled quickly out the door and onto the ice.

A few hours of sitting and waiting are enough to make you appreciate the patience required to excel at this sport. A fisherman named Clark Chapman loaned me the use of his shanty and spear, and I spent part of one morning wondering what I would do if a sturgeon swam into view. Sturgeon meat is said to be delicious. The steaks, cubed and deep-fried in oil, are supposed to taste like lobster. Still, I had doubts. How, for instance, do you clean a hundred-pound fish that doesn't have a skeleton and whose skin is often compared to leather?

By my watch it was 8:05 A.M. The spear rested on a piece of bent wire lipped over the edge of the large hole in the shanty's floor. The cord was arranged in a neat, loose coil beside the hole, well away from feet and equipment. I adjusted the gas heater, settled down on a bench, and leaned slightly forward to watch. The water in Black Lake is obscured by suspended particulate matter. To make a dark fish more visible, Clark Chapman had dropped potato peelings to the bottom. Magnified by the water, they glowed ghostly white on the bottom. No other details were visible down there, though just below the ice a fine mist of algae drifted steadily past, carried by the lake's slight current. It was 8:07. I opened the door a crack and looked out into the sudden, glaring whiteness. A light snow fell, the flakes drifting at angles to the ice. Shanties scattered around me appeared to be mostly deserted.

I closed the door and waited a minute or two for my vision to adjust. The interior of a shanty must remain as dark as possible, and it is only gradually that the dim light rising from the hole reaches high enough to illuminate the interior. I poured a cup of coffee and set the cup to cool on the floor beside my feet. I brought the decoy up, winding the line on a large spool mounted on the ceiling, and when the decoy was suspended dripping above the water I spun it a hundred or so revolutions clockwise, as I had been instructed by Boyd Crist, until the cord knotted up like the rubber band on a toy airplane propeller. When I lowered the decoy near bottom it hung there, unwinding slowly. If I lifted the cord slightly the decoy rocked, like a red-and-white bird in a pique of indignation. I imagined the activity would enrage a muskie or northern pike and (perhaps) interest a sturgeon. I waited. The water remained lifeless, and I wasn't entirely sure I wanted it otherwise. It was 8:18.

I did not last the entire morning. While eating an early lunch in the circus tent I talked to a Detroit auto worker who admitted he had been coming up to Black Lake to rent shanties for eight years in succession and had yet to see his first sturgeon. Several times he had used shanties that gave up fish to other anglers during the week, but he himself was always limited to fishing on the weekends. "Maybe when the lake is quieter the fish move around more," he speculated. "I'm thinking about taking my entire vacation up here next winter, though I don't know if my wife will go for it."

"Honest now," I asked. "Why do you do it?"

He paused a moment, stroking his chin. "I like sitting in the shanty. It gives me time to think."

A Vendetta

There is a certain sweeping bend on the lower Boardman River, a place of deep water and drowned logs, where the river slows to mull in gloomy introspection. Upstream and down are shallows: slow, sandy flats interspersed with hummocks of aquatic weeds, where small brown trout sometimes splash after mayfly duns. The bend—or, as I always think of it, the Bend, capitalized— offers the only substantial hiding place for trout in that stretch of river. Yet I rarely find trout there. Consequently I have always dreamed the place was home to elusive browns of unlikely size, that I was the only person in the world who suspected it, and that someday, on one of those rare and fecund mornings when every fish in the river is eager to feed without caution, I will cast a fly there and raise a monster.

Well, it happened. A rare morning in July. The right fly, the right moment. And truly, a monster.

I'm not sure how to define it precisely, but there are certain days when you know you must get on the water, any water, as soon as possible. It might simply be a matter of sunlight. Summer can be so ruthlessly bright and cloudless that it is useless to fish except very early or very late in the day. When you wake to find the sky low and glowering, the air heavy with impending rain, it is cause for rejoicing. Phone in sick to work, make excuses, lie to your spouse—just get to some water.

I live less than a twenty-minute drive from the Bend. It is not secret water. During the week I usually have it to myself, but on weekends it can be crowded with a half-dozen anglers, each of them no doubt immersed in his own fantasy, none of them, to my knowledge, catching a fish to satisfy it. It is a place people seem to fish from habit, because it is inviting and pleasant and should hold fish. The banks are well trodden; forked sticks rise from the water's edge like oversized wishbones.

That morning in July, with the sky low and motionless and the faintest mist in the air, the water seemed to moan and

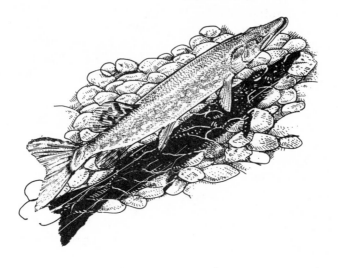

shiver with vitality. Even the light was unusual—somehow alive, vibrant. No trout fed on the surface, there were no clues I could describe, yet even before I made the first cast, I knew, I knew . . .

Near the upstream beginning of the Bend a steep, wooded bank drops straight to the water. Some mornings, when the light allows it, you can cling to the trees above and look straight into the pool and see the bottom as clearly as if you were viewing it through a glass-bottomed boat. Every log and stick, every cobblestone and patch of yellow sand stands out in magnified detail, washed by the languid and ephemeral shadows of the current. But not a single living creature is in sight.

I approached from upstream, walking on the narrow strip of gravel below the bank, crouching when I neared the deep water. At the edge of it a short point of gravel turns the current toward midstream, creating a deep pool and an eddy. The water there circles in a casual spin cycle that traps a perpetual rotating raft of scum and leaves and drowned insects. I know from peering into the river from the bank above that the deepest water is there, and that the bottom is tangled with roots and sunken branches. It is a place for large fish.

Crouched on the shore, I backcast once and dropped a muddler minnow in the center of the eddy. The fly floated for a moment, joining the merry-go-round of debris. I twitched it and it sank. I twitched it again, causing the fly to dart forward, humping the water slightly and leaving a small wake. I retrieved it rapidly. At the precise moment the fly came into sight, swimming an inch below the surface and nearly to the protection of the gravel bar, the monster struck.

It came from the deep water at the edge of the gravel bar, appearing so suddenly it might have been launched in warfare. In one sudden, deadly, graceful motion it engulfed the fly, arched its flank, swirled the water, and disappeared into the depths again. I saw clearly the long snout, the spear shape, the green bars: a northern pike. It sliced my line so cleanly I didn't feel it.

It should not have been a surprise. Less than a mile

downstream the river empties into a shallow, weed-filled lake where northern pike are the dominant game fish. Marv Saxton, an old friend who occasionally fishes the river at night during the hex hatch, once cast repeatedly to a large fish that was cruising back and forth over the width of the river, feeding noisily, swirling the surface, making an arrogant spectacle unlike anything he had ever witnessed in the Boardman. When Marv finally hooked and landed the thing it proved to be a six-pound pike so stuffed with duns and spinners its belly was slung deep as a bass's.

The proper attitude, I suppose, would have been alarm. Northern pike are an unwelcome addition to a trout stream. The general prejudice is that they are evidence of a declining neighborhood. Let one in and the next thing you know there are dozens of them, the trout disappear, and the river is taken over by pike, smallmouth bass, perch, and catfish.

Yet, I was intrigued. I have always been fascinated by pike. I admire their pure gangland violence, their skill as predators, the reckless way they attack. They are unpredictable and dauntless. They grow to frightening size. Besides, I was raised in a family of pike fishermen. In my father's and uncles' hierarchy of value, pike ruled. They were followed closely in importance by largemouth bass and, a big step down, by walleyes. Trout were a little too fancy for my family's taste. Perch and bluegills could fill an otherwise fishless afternoon, but they were not serious game. Only pike, and the stories about big ones caught and lost, could put a light in my uncles' eyes and make them sit up straight in their chairs to listen.

The stories were as colorful as myths, and had grown polished with many tellings. They talked about a day many years ago when Tony Mikowski, a wiry old Pole who was a friend of the family, was fishing alone in the narrows connecting North and South Lake Leelanau. He had cast a large spoon toward the pilings that lined the narrow channel and when he retrieved it, got snagged on a log. But the log swam slowly away, towing Tony and his rowboat the length of the channel out into the open water of the south lake. The fight took forty-five minutes. An ancient photo shows a young, wry-looking Tony holding the pike with both hands: The head is at his chin, the tail rests on the ground.

In the 1950s and 1960s my father and my uncle, Eldon Blough, often cast plugs for largemouth bass from an old, wooden rowboat they kept chained to a tree on the shore of South Bar Lake near the village of Empire. One afternoon, my father was about to lift his red-and-white Bass-Oreno from the water to make another cast when an enormous pike streaked in, grabbed the lure the way a dog might grab a stick, and shook it. The strike broke my father's line. The northern remained in place, suspended slightly below the surface beside the boat, resting there as if nothing of importance had just occurred. It was an enormous fish, as long as the boat was wide—four feet, by later measurement—with the broad back and heavy midsection of a predator accustomed to doing what it pleased. Eldon could only say, "Look at the size of that son of a bitch," repeating himself over and over in disbelief. When it swam off, the lure still visible in its mouth, my father declared it the largest northern pike he had ever seen—alive, mounted, or in photographs.

The pike I saw in the Boardman River measured no more than thirty inches and weighed perhaps eight pounds—too small for family mythology—but the old feelings it stirred were too strong to resist. I drove home, traded my fly rod for a spinning rod, and returned to the river prepared to do battle. If I did not capture this fish it might sire a brood of deadly, arrowlike savages predisposed to feed on young trout. Gail, who complains because I seldom bring home fish for the table, would be delighted with the armload of fillets I dropped in the sink. In one swift act I would be righteous citizen, conservationist, provider, hero, and heir to family tradition.

I tied a four-inch Rapala to my line, flipped it into the eddy, and retrieved it less than twelve inches when I saw the flash and the swelling surge and felt the solid rap of the strike. The hooks missed. I cast again, but the pike, like a hook-stung trout, refused to rise.

I cut the Rapala off, tied on a small lead-headed jig, and threaded a rubber twister tail on the hook. It plopped in the eddy, sank to the bottom, and I brought it back slowly, raising and lowering it with my rod-tip, manipulating it just fast enough to activate the tail. When it was nearly to the gravel bar I had an impression of vicious activity deep in the pool. I struck but the line went limp, sheered off cleanly above the knot.

In the days that followed I fished the pool with dozens of plugs, spoons, spinners, and jigs. I drifted lip-hooked shiners through the eddy, bottom-fished with dead smelt and crayfish, gurgled top-water lures on the surface, dragged crankbaits through the depths. I began to suspect I had imagined the fish. Maybe someone else had caught it. Possibly, long association with brown trout had taught it to be leader-shy and reclusive. I fished on overcast days and on bright days, at dawn, at noon, at night. No day came along as rich and promising as that first had been, no moment was as electrifying. Still, the pike, if it was there, had to feed sometime. I should have caught it. There was no reason why I, a seasoned and relatively patient angler, could not catch one medium-sized northern pike living in my favorite trout river.

The last day of the season, September 30, with yellow leaves drifting downstream like a routed armada, I retrieved a large gold spinner deep along the bottom of the pool and caught a sixteen-inch brown trout. It was a typical trout for the Boardman—marked in brilliant autumn colors, with the plump body and small head of a healthy fish. It was, I realized later, one of the finest trout I caught that year.

Even as I unhooked the trout and steadied it in the current I thought of the season to come and wondered if minnows drifted through the pool in the high, discolored water of April might be effective. The pike would be a pound or two heavier, no doubt wiser and meaner.

I released the trout and climbed the bank above the river. Hanging to the trunks of saplings for support, I peered into the pool. It was as clear and revealing as an aquarium. At first I saw nothing but bottom debris and contours, the shifting lines of the current. Then I saw the pike. It rested motionless on the bottom, streamlined and camouflaged, serene as a malevolent sage. My heart pounded with excitement. As I watched, the pike rose from the bottom and turned, spooked by my shadow perhaps, and drifted downstream into darker water. I did not try casting to it. I was content to wait. By next season it would have forgotten the hazards of artificial lures. All winter it would be there, growing, dreaming of trout.

AFTER RAIN

My sons were playing war the day I met the new neighbor. He was about forty, I guessed, a quiet, dark-haired man with a good mustache and sad eyes. We lived in a quiet, tree-shaded neighborhood in the old part of Traverse City, in a house with a front porch where Gail and I could sit and watch the kids play. Aaron ran around the corner of the house making sounds of explosions and gunfire with his mouth, then fell on the front lawn in a raging parody of death. The neighbor, on his own porch, watched him. He smiled at me and shook his head as if sorry for the innocence he and I had somehow lost.

"Happier days?" I asked.

"Well, they aren't what they used to be."

We were both fishermen, we learned, and had grown

up prowling small creeks in the area searching for brook trout. The trout and the creeks and the way we fished them—with worms and split shot—were best suited for small boys, we agreed, but we had never outgrown them. The neighbor, Wayne, suggested I join him sometime on a stream close by. He did not say when. Weeks passed.

One night, after a day of humidity and stillness, the wind rose suddenly from the west, strong enough to shake windows and shear branches from the trees in the yard. The power failed. Thunder and lightning began cracking in simultaneous barrages, and Gail and the kids went to the basement with flashlights and a radio. I invented reasons to stay upstairs. Before the rain obscured the windows I watched the world frozen in lightning strobes: trees in violent dance, clouds that looked like exploding cities. During one flash I glanced at the neighbor's house and saw Wayne framed there, in his window, watching the sky.

In the morning the world was whole again, the sky cleansed and blue. I spent the day replacing shingles on the roof and gathering branches from the yard. Wayne came home from work late in the afternoon and called across the fence to suggest we go fishing. "Sometimes it's best after rain," he said.

He had a passion for small waters that had condensed to purity: He fished only with bait, for trout, on two streams that wound through tiny, undeveloped valleys barely outside the city limits and emptied into the Boardman River a half-mile from one another. His job, driving truck for a concrete manufacturer, kept him so busy in the summer that he needed trout water that was convenient. The creeks held both brook trout and brown trout and were not often fished. I had crossed over them hundreds of time and never given them a second look.

We fished his favorite of the creeks from its mouth, where it ended at the river, upstream toward the highway. Wayne proved to be good company, considerate and solicitous, showing off the stream proudly. He fished with refreshing concentration, as if nothing else mattered, pausing occasionally to point out places where he had taken trout on other days, communicating in a few whispered words or in low, restrained gestures. But mostly he just fished, calmly and with confidence, stepping quietly among bogs and cedar clumps or standing absolutely still to watch the creek.

When he found a spot he liked he moved silently to within casting range and lobbed a night crawler upstream. The bait drifted on the bottom past tiny cutbanks hidden behind trailing weeds. They were places I would not have bothered fishing. I was in the habit of trying only those holes deep enough to provide obvious cover, and there seemed to be no cover at all in many of the places where Wayne fished. Yet trout up to twelve inches long darted from beneath the banks to grab his bait. He kept a pair of brown trout for supper and released the others carefully.

At a deep hole—I was in comfortable territory again—I crawled on my hands and knees until I could reach the water with the tip of my rod. It was the most promising spot in a half-mile of water, the stream tumbling over an ancient, sunken log into a pool that looked to be chest deep. A week earlier Wayne had hooked a brown trout here, he said, that leaped to eye level, landed on the far side of a deadfall, and broke his four-pound-test leader. He estimated it measured eighteen inches, perhaps more. I flipped my night crawler into the current and let it wash into the depths. It drifted out of the pool into the shallows at the end and I cast again. After a few tries I eased out of the way to let Wayne take my place.

On his second cast he had a strike deep in the pool. His rod arched sharply for a moment, then straightened. He shrugged and grinned. "The mysterious ways of trout," he whispered.

We stayed there for a while, resting on the damp ground beneath the cedars, chatting about our jobs and our families. Earlier we had flushed a grouse and Wayne had watched the bird's thundering flight as if he longed for a twenty-gauge. Now I asked if he hunted. The question seemed to distress him. I suspected I was going to hear a lecture, but he said only that he gave up gun sports years ago.

"Why?"

"I guess I'd seen enough shooting," he said.

He stood and started walking away upstream. "Try the water at this bend," he called back. "I'll go on ahead a ways."

The creek divided into several tangled channels around the bend. I cast my bait into a spillage of side current, where it flowed past gnarled roots into a tiny pool. The water in the pool was deep enough to appear black and circled lazily, as if drawn down into a drain. My night crawler undulated in the current, then sank into the pool and was immediately struck by a trout. The rod bowed for a second, but the trout was small, less than nine inches, and I lifted it easily from the water. It was hooked lightly and I released it.

We made slow progress upstream, occasionally passing each other, sometimes fishing opposite sides of the creek. Wayne seemed to catch trout everywhere, while I could find them only in the deepest holes. I caught a pair of barely legal brook trout, but nothing of size.

The light was nearly gone by the time we reached the culvert below the road embankment. Wayne said that early in the season he had caught a three-pound rainbow there, perhaps a stray steelhead that had come up the Boardman from Lake Michigan and worked its way into the stream. Now he invited me to try the pool, pointing to the white lip of foam where the flow tumbled from the culvert, then explaining how the current bent away, forming a deep hole along the far bank. I flipped my bait where he pointed and hooked another nine-inch brown. When I cast again I misjudged in the darkness and wrapped my line around a branch near the culvert. I broke off and we climbed the embankment to the highway.

In the truck Wayne let traffic clear before pulling onto the road. I waited a moment, then asked him what kind of shooting would make a person give up hunting. His face, lit by the green dash lamp, was immobile; he stared at the road with no expression at all.

"Sorry. None of my business," I said.

"No, it's all right," he said. "The Vietnamese kind."

"I don't suppose you found many trout over there."

He laughed. "None to speak of."

We stopped at the traffic light at South Airport Road. In the last year mini markets and gas stations had sprung up on two of the four corners. Friends of mine had once hunted pheasants in the fields that used to be here.

The light changed and Wayne shifted through the gears. "It's not a big deal," he said. "Sometimes I don't like to talk about it because people have weird ideas on the subject. I never know how they feel, and talking about it becomes more effort than it's worth. But like I say, I don't consider it a big deal anymore. I was a G.I. in Vietnam in '67 and '68 and was there through the Tet offensive. I don't know how much you know about it."

"Just what I've read. That it was hairy."

"It was. We got our tails twisted. I lost some friends. At the end of it I figured I'd seen enough, but it wasn't over for me yet. Two weeks before I was scheduled to come home I took a small-arms round through the side of my helmet. It knocked me to the ground and left a six-inch welt across my scalp like I'd been seared with a blowtorch. I thought I was dying, or already dead, lying there with my face in the mud. When I got home I discovered I'd sort of lost interest in noisy sports."

"So you decided to concentrate on small streams and trout."

"Right."

I wanted to say more. I wanted to tell him that I sympathized, that I hated the fickleness of public opinion and the way Hollywood turned him into a hero two decades after the fact, that I knew at some approximate level what it must have been like for him over there.

But of course I didn't know. How could I? I was hardly more than a child then, flexing my father's fly rod in the living room while Walter Cronkite listed casualty figures on television. Wayne was slashing through jungles on reconnaissance patrol while I carried a 30-30 Winchester for the first time, hunting deer with my father and uncles in eighty acres of Michigan hardwoods. While I sat dreaming in an oak forest, intoxicated by the scent of autumn leaves, Wayne laid stunned in the mud on the other side of the world, his nostrils full of the rank, earthy smell of eternity. I could not even imagine what he knew.

"Guess I've led a sheltered life," I said.

"Count your blessings."

There was nothing more I could say. We were almost home. I thought of Aaron and Nick playing war games in the yard, and started counting.

WIDE MARGINS

When we're discouraged by the madness of the world and need to involve ourselves in something elemental, we turn to water. This is a significant and perhaps universal urge, I think, and makes an excellent excuse to go fishing. Last night, more discouraged than usual, I set the alarm for early, almost the middle of the night. I wanted to be in the water before daylight.

Now it is a half-hour before sunrise, not yet day and no longer night, and I'm walking through the sand in my waders toward the mouth of the Platte River. The air is as fresh as spring water. I can smell Lake Michigan and although there is no wind I hear the low, quiet sounds of big water, as if the lake were breathing easily in sleep. It is April first—early enough for fools; too early, I hope, for other fishermen.

The trail leads past a low ridge of dunes, the sand here so deep and yielding I sink to the ankles. From the broad upper beach I can see the lake. It is calm this early in the day, the water rising and falling gently. I step into the shallows, gravel shifting beneath me, stones grinding stones, then step deeper to where the bottom is smooth with sand and as hard and flat as pavement. I move slowly in the water, conscious of the small waves pushed ahead by my legs.

Three fishermen are here already. They stand motionless as herons, waist deep in the lake, watching rods they have propped on holders pushed into the bottom. I had hoped to be alone but am not disappointed; sharing this much water is easy. I wade out to a place beside them and they each turn to look at me. One nods. "Morning gentlemen," I say.

The lake is big, stretching away to vague horizons, but we stand only ten or fifteen feet apart to fish the best water straight out from the river, where the current spilling into the lake has dug a channel perhaps two feet deeper than the surrounding bottom. I fish with a spinning rod baited with a small bag of trout roe. I know the others use spawn for bait as well, and that their bait, like mine, is weighted with enough split shot to make a long cast possible but not so much that the bait is anchored to bottom. The others tend two rods each, propped up on the holders so that they rise

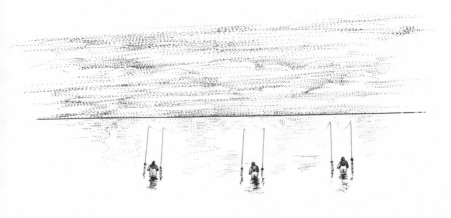

straight up from the water. They watch their rod tips attentively; a strike can be gentle, the softest bump. Our baits rest on the bottom, like nuggets waiting for miners to nudge them with their toes.

Another man wades out from shore and takes a place in line with us. He casts his bait far out into the lake and holds his rod lightly and expectantly in his hand. Then an older man and his grown son come, both wearing yellow rain jackets with the hoods up, as if they are expecting rain. I look at the sky but it is empty of clouds and changing from black to shades of deep blue. Behind us the horizon is washed in violet with a band of rose just above the hills. Morning is materializing around us.

We are here because in April the mouths of Lake Michigan tributaries can be crowded with schools of smelt, gizzard shade, alewives, and other bait fish, which attract steelhead, brown trout, lake trout, and salmon. The trout and salmon often come in clusters—pods of fish of similar size that cruise the shoreline, homing in on the rivers like sharks on a blood scent. The hour before and after dawn is usually the best fishing of the day, but this morning, so far, there have been no strikes.

The lake has turned the color of pewter. As the sky lightens the horizon pulls away, becoming so distant I think of Thoreau's "I love a wide margin to my life." People who have never seen the Great Lakes are surprised to see how enormous they are. From here the Wisconsin shore is more than fifty miles away, far beyond the curve of the earth. Cross that distance by boat and much of the way you will be out of sight of land and can easily believe you're on an ocean rather than a lake.

We stand motionless, waiting. The cold water numbs my legs, even through insulated waders, wool pants, and polypropylene underwear. This is fishing that requires patience. I usually prefer more active versions of the sport. I like to move, to cast to feeding fish or search for inviting places where fish might be hiding. This has more in common with bait fishing for catfish than most forms of trout fishing.

But in certain moods it is satisfying. I once stood near a fisherman at the mouth of another river who remained still for so long that a sparrow fluttered to a landing on the top of his bald head, apparently mistaking him for a wooden piling. It's possible to become so serene you turn inanimate.

Somebody in the line of fishermen says, "Cold." Another answers, "Not as cold as last week." One of the men who was already fishing when I arrived shifts on his feet and begins the day's first story:

"Guy I work with, Bob Stewart, was fishing the mouth of the Boardman two weeks ago. Middle of the day and he was there all alone, on his lunch break from work, not another soul in sight. Bob figured it must be too early for the run, since nobody else was fishing, but what the hell, he had an hour to kill. Waded out there all alone and cast a spawn bag and right away caught a three-pound steelhead. He didn't have a stringer with him and he didn't want to walk all the way back to shore so he dropped the trout in a plastic garbage bag and shoved it down inside his waders. He cast again and caught another one the same size, and shoved that one down his waders too. The next couple casts he had hits but missed them, then lost one, and finally caught one more the size of the first two before it was time to get back to work. He wades to shore holding up his waders with both hands because of the weight of the fish in them and there's a guy standing on the beach watching him. The guy asks him if he caught anything and Bob says, 'Nah, not even a hit.' At that moment, with the guy standing there five feet away already looking at him like he didn't believe him, the trout start flopping to beat hell. Bob's waders are bouncing like a gunny sack full of rabbits. He says, 'Musta been something I ate,' then walks on up the bank to his truck."

There's quiet laughter. If the fishing was better we would have little need to talk. But now one story is traded for another, as surely as merchandise. The younger of the men in the yellow rain jackets speaks up:

"I hooked a sturgeon once at the mouth of the Boardman. I was fishing for steelhead at the time and figured I had the world's record trout when it first hit. Took a spawn bag and marshmallow and just ran and ran. I was with a buddy in a boat, luckily, or I never would have seen what I was hooked to. We pulled up anchor and followed it with the trolling motor for about an hour before it tired and came up to the surface. Big old black thing as long as a submarine. Must of weighed eighty pounds. We didn't know what the hell to do with it so we cut the line down by the hook and watched that big sonofabitch roll over and sink out of sight."

One of the three who was here when I arrived says, "Biggest fish I ever seen caught in the Great Lakes was right here where we're standing, in the fall of 1984. A king salmon thirty-eight and a half pounds on six-pound-test line. Took the guy about forty-five minutes to land and he sat down afterwards in the sand holding that fish in his arms like it was the biggest and slimiest baby you ever seen."

Someone laughs. "I was fishing here last fall," he says, "talking to a fellow from downstate who'd come up on his vacation to fish the salmon run. I'll be damned if a Chinook about twenty or twenty-five pounds didn't come barrelling up the way they do sometimes in shallow water, launch itself in the air, and smack that guy square in the chest. It knocked him on his ass in the water and filled his waders. He stumbled around splashing and cussing, trying to get back on his feet. It looked like the poor bastard had been *torpedoed*."

The talk dwindles, each of us thinking his own thoughts. The fisherman beside me pulls a Thermos from the back of his fishing vest and pours a cup of coffee. He offers me a sip.

The current spirals in tiny eddies far out into Lake Michigan. You can't cast far enough to reach the limits of the current, even if you have waded to the tops of your waders and are bouncing slowly on your toes to keep above the slight, breathlike cadence of the swells. Yet everyone casts as far as they can. We want to exceed ourselves, to push our boundaries. This simple physical act is one way to take measure of the vastness of the lake.

Later, with the sun up and warming our backs, one of the fishermen grabs his rod and heaves back on it. The rod bends deeply for a moment, throbbing, then goes into a deeper bend as the fish runs. It runs and runs. It runs long past the point when most fish in the Great Lakes would slow or turn or come to the surface. It runs straight out toward the center of the lake, toward the indistinct line of the horizon, toward Wisconsin. It could be racing toward the edge of the earth. It runs until the efficiently turning spool of the man's reel begins to show bare metal and the line on it is reduced to a few turns. The fisherman puts all the pressure he dares on the fish. But it continues to run.

Afterward the man is shaking his head, rattled by the size of the fish he has lost. Already he is composing the story for later telling. It occurs to me that on this beach we are standing on the boundary between what is safe and known and what is perilous and unknown. If so, we stand waist deep in risk. We are beach walkers, attracted to peril. We need wide margins to our lives.

THE DUNES
IN WINTER

As a child I sometimes tried to imagine how the world would look if every step taken by every person who had ever lived was printed immutably in ink. City sidewalks would be black as typewriter ribbons, and the countryside would be braided with aimless, tangled trails. But somewhere—in the hardwoods behind our house, in the tiny forgotten valleys beyond the dunes—I was sure there would be a few small patches of earth free of prints. I would search for those places, claim them for my own, and become the first person in the history of the earth to stand in them.

Thirty miles from my home is a tourist lookout at Sleeping Bear Dunes where you can stand on a platform and see wooded hills to the east and an impressive view of Lake Michigan to the west. During the summer it's a popular place to go for picnics and day hikes, for throwing Frisbees, letting the dogs run, taking photographs on the bluff with the blue lake in the background. In winter it's seldom visited. After the first snows, the access road to the area is blocked off and becomes an informal ski trail. It's not a trail of interest to serious skiers, since it is not groomed and tends to become sinuous and rutted with the converging lines of many tracks. On the windswept stretches the snow remains so thin that ski poles often slip against the road's asphalt.

At the end of the road, past the padlocked restrooms and the stacks of chained picnic tables, are several miles of dunes extending in a blunt point into Lake Michigan. Winds ravage the dunes during the winter and keep all but the most determined visitors away. The snow there is mixed too thoroughly with sand to be skied, the two substances blended together by the wind and thrown into elegant, variegated drifts. To travel in the dunes you must shoulder your skis and trudge through the sand and snow, finding protection from the wind only in a few scattered clumps of aspens, where the trees are stunted and bent awkwardly to the south. Other people may have been here, but their trails have been erased by the scrubbing of wind and sand. It's a place that reminds you of your impermanence.

Here you have no difficulty finding solitude. Even most mammals and birds have abandoned the dunes, migrating to the protected alder swamps and spruce and hemlock stands in the lowlands. Tracks of white-tailed deer are sometimes visible in the narrow gullies, where the buds of young aspen attract them, but the trails are always solitary and meandering, perhaps made by experienced bucks that sought refuge during hunting season and found no reason to leave.

I've thought often of those bucks. When I was fifteen and sixteen, my first deer seasons, I hunted with my father and uncles in the woods adjacent to the dunes. The first day of the first year stands out clearly. I remember stepping from the car into thick, fertile darkness so complete it masked even sound, striding beside my father, feeling the nose-aching cold, the satisfying heft of the 30–30. We walked until we reached a large stump far inside the woods. The northern Michigan woods are dotted with such stumps—ancient, bleached pine, rotted from the center out, remnants of magnificent forests that were clear-cut eighty years ago.

My father poured two cups of coffee from the Thermos. We sipped quietly in the darkness, without talking, then he guided me to one side of the stump and showed me where to sit. He took a position beside me. Other days I would be on my own, but now, this first morning, we would stay together.

Even then, more than twenty years ago, the rural corners of our state were vanishing. Subdivisions sliced the land into lucrative pieces of pie, new roads and cul-de-sacs appeared, woodlands where just a few years earlier my father had hunted were now marked off by surveyor's stakes. Every season there was more competition for hunting space. Lines of automobiles, each filled with red-coated hunters, had been entering our county for days. My father said we would have to hunt far from the road if we expected to hunt alone.

So we had parked on a two-track logging trail five miles off the highway, and walked another mile into the woods to this stump at the edge of a field. We seemed to have found a place as remote as northern Ontario, a place that was wild and unbounded. We were sure to be the only hunters for miles around. When dawn came I expected to see enormous, thick-antlered bucks grazing without concern where the meadow blended into the woods.

What I saw instead were hunters. In that first gray light, with darkness disintegrating around us, the blaze orange of hunters' jackets stood out like bonfires. One hunter, a few hundred yards away, glassed the field with binoculars. Another, closer, appeared to be asleep at the base of a small maple. Yet another, dressed in a one-piece suit and wearing earmuffs, waved to us.

My father stood in disgust. He waited until he had caught the eye of each man, not risking a careless movement that could be misinterpreted by an over-eager hunter, then with me at his heels led the way back to the car.

The remainder of that season, and the next, we hunted with permission on private land in Day Forest, adjacent to the dunes. The forest, dense with second-growth oak and maple, was relatively uncrowded. One morning I sat at the base of an oak and watched two young does pick their way through the underbrush, walking with the dainty concern of small girls in dancing shoes. Unaware of my presence, they passed so close I could have touched them with my rifle. Another time, pausing to look over one of the juniper-spotted meadows at the foot of the dunes, I saw a buck trotting a quarter-mile away, carrying its bulk of antlers in what can only be described as a regal manner.

One noon, while we drove from Day Forest to my Uncle Bob Schmidt's house for lunch, we pulled off the road just as a ten-point buck dashed across Bob's driveway in front of us into the woods. We laughed that we would see such a white-tail, the largest of the season, in such a place. Then we were quiet, thinking of where that buck was going. My uncle's house was literally in the shadow of the dunes, situated at the base of its easternmost bluff, and the deer had been running directly for the dunes.

We knew there were men who hunted up there. They were loners, skilled at tracking and stalking, and they knew how to keep their mouths shut. If they found trophy deer they never admitted it, but we heard rumors and speculated that large, experienced bucks would abandon the heavily hunted lowlands and take refuge in the wooded swales scattered across the dunes. I had visited some of those swales in the summer and found them dark and cool, shaded by poplar and carpeted with sedge grass and wildflowers. Some were fed by tiny springs, with water that seeped into the sand almost as soon as it emerged from the ground.

Yet we never entered the dunes during hunting season. Everyone talked about going there, but there were problems of access, and the difficulties of hunting open land where you would be visible for hundreds of yards in every direction. I understood, too, that my father and my uncles chose to honor the place as a sanctuary. I felt no such obligation but was too young to hunt on my own that year, and in later years would be distracted by other places and other game. Always, in the back of my mind, I thought of the dunes as a place to find trophy whitetails, a place I would hunt another time. Now I too think of it as a sanctuary.

Near the crest of the dunes fresh deer tracks lead toward a swale, visible only as a cluster of treetops above the sand, and I imagine the deer bedded there, near water and browse, protected from the wind. The dunes and Day Forest are under the jurisdiction of a national park now, and will never be hauled away or subdivided. In exchange, the area has been bounded by boardwalks, parking lots, and information pavilions. Hunting is allowed, on a limited basis, but it has recently come under attack and has inspired a bitter exchange of letters to the editor of our local newspaper.

Snow squalls rush across the open lake. They come from the north, as far away as I can see, and pass beyond sight to the south. The squalls seem to be in migration, like flocks of white birds so tightly patterned no individuals can be seen, the flocks swarming after each other in mysterious clans, enormous as clouds, riding the wind toward grace and warm weather. As they pass, square-mile patches of the lake are obliterated, the whitecaps dissolving slowly into whiteness. Lake freighters, if they sailed this time of year, could never emerge from those squalls unchanged.

Occasionally the bruised clouds separate and shafts of sunlight descend at angles to the water, spotlighting the waves. My mother grew up near the base of the dunes in the resort town of Glen Arbor, and knows the lake well. In the quiet days of her youth it was her primary source of entertainment. Even in summer, when resorters from Chicago and Detroit filled the cottages and hotels and gathered at the public beaches, she had the lake mostly to herself. When I was very young and we visited Glen Arbor to walk the shore, she told me the sudden, angled shafts of light over the lake were known as Jacob's ladder and it was possible to climb them to heaven if you knew how. I remember being entranced, but dubious.

From the top of the bluff I can see the uneven fringe of pack ice along the shore 450 feet below. The ice covers the narrow beach like an undulating, trackless road. Even from this height streaks of sand are visible on the snow. I can see too where waves have formed grotesque sculptures, crevasses, and occasional ice bridges. Blow spouts appear where surging waves have carved passages through the ice, their spurting water constructing volcanolike cones as tall as a man. The water near shore is suspended with slushy ice the consistency of margaritas, causing the waves to become muted and sluggish. They swell toward the ice, rise slowly against its face, and recede. After a moment, always longer than expected, the cones erupt with geysers, like the exhalations of whales. I remember that some days, if it has been very cold, you can find fallen drops frozen into odd-shaped pearlies and cat's-eyes of ice.

When my brother and I were old enough to explore the Glen Arbor beaches alone, while my parents visited relatives, we were allowed to go there only after promising to avoid the spout holes and their tunnels. The adults worried that we would slip or be flushed into the lake, where five minutes immersion would be fatal. We promised to be careful.

At first we followed the shore, over ice that extended far up the beach like buckled pavement and threatened, some years, to topple the lifeguard's tower and invade the netless tennis courts. Snow, dusted over the ice, was untracked as far as we could see, possible evidence that our parents were right about the hazards of the place. We walked cautiously at first, afraid the ice would collapse. When our confidence grew we ran, as best we could on the slippery ice, sliding down the slopes, twirling like clumsy, heavily dressed ballet dancers.

We were drawn inevitably to the tunnels and approached them obliquely, as if we had no intention of going near them. They varied in size. Some were too small to enter, others the width of culverts, a few large enough to stand inside. All were worn smooth as blown glass by the scouring water. If the sun shone, their interiors glowed with a crystal-blue light and you could see, suspended in the ice many feet away, spiraling strings of bubbles and grains of quartz. We hacked at the blue ice with pocketknives; in our hands the chips lost their color, became transparent, and we put them in our mouths to suck like candy. Squatting in the tunnels, watching the downhill slant to the queer blue light of the lake, we felt as daring as arctic explorers, as accomplished as mountain climbers.

On the dunes now I am content to accept quieter satisfactions. I've learned to find pleasure in small things, in unpredictable moments, in the discovery of forgotten places. It's my good fortune to be surrounded by an abundance of such places. The lake, the dunes, the shoreline far below the bluff—I had forgotten them all. Sitting in the ice-spangled sand, in the wind, witnessing Jacob's ladder and the erasure of snow squalls, I become optimistic again. It's possible to believe there is space enough for everyone.

BRIDGES

On a lake as large as Long Lake it is unusual to meet the neighbors who live on the far shore. The distance across—a mile or more, most places—reduces their lives to an insignificant scale, like looking down on them from an airplane. When we boat past one another's houses we do not stare openly, the way summer visitors do; we avert our eyes out of respect for whatever privacy remains.

But the island is neutral ground. On maps the small, round, vigorously wooded islet at the north end of the lake is labeled "Brush Island," but to everyone who lives in the area it is "Anne's Island," named by a Detroit lawyer who owned a cottage next to my parents' house and bought the island decades ago as a gift for his daughter. The lawyer is dead now and Anne is grown and married and spends her

winters on the East Coast, but the island is still hers and remains unposted and undeveloped, an inviting spot for picnics and morning expeditions.

Aaron, Nick, and I were wading barefoot in the shallows around the island one day, looking for fossils, when we noticed an old man rowing across the lake in a wooden boat. The boat caught my eye immediately. It was unusual to see nonmotorized craft other than sailboats on our lake, let alone a wooden boat with natural finish, a boat that appeared, even from a half-mile distant, so elegant it must have been hand-built by an artisan. I watched as it drew nearer, curious about the man who would own such a craft. He rowed steadily, turning occasionally to gauge his distance from the shore. He had white hair that lifted and fell in the breeze, and the deeply tanned skin of a sailor or farmer. I supposed he was in his sixties or seventies.

He beached his boat on the sand spit at the south end of the island, shipping his oars gently. My sons and I stood, knee deep in the water, watching him. He nodded at me, without interest I thought, and at the boys, whose arms were loaded by then with beach stones, odd bits of driftwood, bones of birds, and a dozen golf balls they had found washed up mysteriously in the shallows. The old man walked into the trees and climbed the bank slowly to the tiny elevated clearing at the center of the island. I could see him through the trees, surveying the lake from there, looking a few moments in each direction. Then he disappeared over the far bank.

From the shore of the island we could look across a quarter-mile of open water to my parents' house, where I lived from the time I was nine until I was twenty-one, and where they still live now. It is a low green house on a small hill, set in an open yard surrounded by woods. There are houses up and down the shore, both directions, though most are hidden at least in part by trees. I remember as a boy standing on our dock focusing on a patch of undeveloped woods across the lake, putting my hands like blinders on either side of my face so I could not see the houses and cottages that lined most of the shore. I pretended I was living in the nineteenth century and seeing the lake for the first time, or that I was in Ontario, hundreds of miles from marinas and water-skiers and walleye tournaments. I imagined myself coming upon Long Lake for the first time, a virgin lake surrounded by wilderness and full of northern pike so large they fed on mallards and muskrats. My own sons seem inclined to similar fantasies, though they have considerably more trouble finding undeveloped stretches of shoreline than I did. The lake has changed in twenty years.

By the time we circled the rest of the island the old man had returned to his boat and pushed off and was rowing steadily away. He faced us as he rowed. Nick, who at four years old was still enchanted with the power of friendly gestures, raised his arm in a farewell wave. The old man let an oar trail for a moment and raised his own arm in answer.

If I had been as trusting as my son I could have talked to the man. I could have told him who we were, where we lived, and how we felt about the island and this lake that has been so important in our lives. I wondered what he thought about the changes he has seen in his lifetime. If I had listened, this is what he might have said:

I *am no curmudgeon. I'm not someone twisted by bitterness, who rants against change. My opinions of the world and our role in it have altered surprisingly little since my youth, when I stood in awe of the progress of mankind, the ingenuity, the spirit, the imagination that has produced such wonders as aircraft and computers and dialysis machines. My sympathies are with Henry Adams, who perceived the electric dynamos of our age as metaphors for the work of a larger hand, symbols of an effort that each generation takes us closer to something like glory. Man's work is triumph over chaos. In the wake of that work, like leaves swirling behind a passing auto, are incidental things. My complaint is with those incidental things.*

The remote lake in northern Michigan where my wife and I built our home forty years ago is now crowded with cottages and bilevel houses. Our simple cedar house is an anomaly, our half-acre yard grotesquely out of proportion to the tiny lots that line the lake now. Not a week passes that we don't get telephone inquiries, or arrive home to find the business cards of realtors tucked inside the screen door. "Call me!" is often written in cheery script across the cards. I drop them, without rancor, into the wastebasket.

In the summer, on my lake, the progress of man loses ground to chaos. It begins Memorial Day weekend with the pleasure boats. Then come water-skiers towed by jet-propelled boats sleek as race cars, piloted by tanned young men who alter the exhausts until the engine noise echoes between the hills with enough violence to crumble mountains. There are hydroplanes and bass boats. There are scuba divers. There are strange, raucous machines like aquatic motorcycles, racing and darting and throwing huge wakes and rooster tails. There are triathletes swimming in legions across the widest portion of the lake.

My lake is no longer my own. After forty years I am not familiar with it, am not welcome on it.

Certain ironies are not lost on me. I consider it significant, for instance, that my life's work was the building of bridges. There was a time, distant now, when the bridges I designed were considered exemplary, even innovative. In small ways I contributed to the progress that has both heartened and disheartened me.

These days I care nothing for literal bridges, for stress factors, suspension systems, or road surfaces. I imagine, instead, that my life and work have been figurative bridges, spanning the passage of two distinct ages. I began work in an age of industrial naivete. When finally I lifted my head from my labors I discovered myself in this modern age, this epoch of wonders.

But still, the incidental things.

Tonight, Andrea sleeps gently, her breath as hushed as the rhythm of wavelets on the beach. I rise from bed quietly, my weight heaving the mattress free. In the living room I dress in trousers, jacket, and boots, then step out into the night.

In the open yard I wait, listening, recalling a thousand nights like this—summer nights when the June bugs pick at window screens and the shore of the lake rings with the chirping and croaking of night creatures. A man my age can sink into memories as easily as into a warm bath. I could take a long breath, close my eyes, and slip beneath the surface, if I chose. I choose not to. I wade through the darkness, down the long sloping yard to the shore of the lake.

The boat is on the bank, turned keel up to repel rain. It is a small wooden skiff built by my grandfather at a time in his life when a winter could be passed in such a way. I know this boat too well to need to see it. I know the varnish is peeling, know the gunwales have become chipped and worn, know the varnish has yellowed where it has become congealed in the slots of brass screws. I lift it upright. The oars are nestled in the sand beneath it, where I left them last night. I find them with my hands, fit them to the locks, then push the wooden hull down the bank until it plows water.

On the lake the border between water and land is defined by shore lights. The lake itself is a bowl of darkness, an inverted, yawning cone of the void. I grip the oars and heft them. They are long and carefully balanced, a fulcrum and lever refined to elegant precision. The locks are worn, carved and polished with use until the wood and metal have acquiesced to agreement, to a kind of marriage. Years ago Andrea and I often rowed this same boat across the lake to the island for picnics, spreading a blanket on the south side, in a spot where the sunlight streamed through oak branches and settled in patches around us. Afterward we went out again in the boat and trolled for bass along the drop-offs. I sat in the center seat, rowing. Andrea sat in the stern holding the rod, watching the line angling away into the water, turning to laugh at me when I became intent, as I always did, on the fishing.

A single stroke of the oars and I am away from shore, gliding into the darkness that covers the lake like a lid. There are no stars tonight, no moon, the sky insulated by heavy clouds. Frogs belch along the shoreline. Crickets rasp their wings in cadence. The murmuring of the oars and locks is as familiar as the whispered voice of my wife.

I bend deep to the oars, my face sternward, and pull as well (I imagine) as any young man. I am young and strong and alone on my lake again. Beneath me the water hisses as it always has. I reach deeper, pull stronger yet, and the boat seems to jump forward, alive as a stallion, and I am rushing across the lake in the darkness, away from my home.

Andrea sleeps in our little house, our sanctuary. With the money we have been offered for it we could live in comfort nearly anywhere. We could buy a cottage on the ocean. We could jettison our possessions, move into a motor home, and pass our remaining years traveling the highways of North America as nomads.

I row. The darkness is so complete it is audible, a background of whisperings to my passing. An illusion of speed is created, of progress. I reach, stretch, pull. Friends who have counseled us say we should leave the lake, leave the congestion and outrageous property taxes, find a place where retirement is easy. I row. The oarlocks whisper, "Never, Never, Never." The water sighs on this lake I cannot own. I row.

I clench my eyes tightly and row.